THE OFFICIAL
CHUCK NORRIS
FACT BOOK

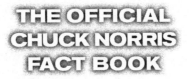

"Chuck Norris is a close friend who I love like a brother (and who once put a choke hold on me at my request, which I immediately regretted). I was delighted to find that *The Official Chuck Norris Fact Book* includes many of the great stories Chuck has told me that I wished others could hear. This book is fun, encouraging, and inspirational. I thoroughly enjoyed it. So will you!"

RANDY ALCORN
author of *Heaven* and *If God Is Good*

THE OFFICIAL CHUCK NORRIS FACT BOOK

101 OF CHUCK'S FAVORITE FACTS AND STORIES

CHUCK NORRIS

with Todd DuBord

Tyndale House Publishers, Inc.

CAROL STREAM, ILLINOIS

Visit Tyndale's exciting Web site at www.tyndale.com.

Visit Chuck Norris's Web site at www.chucknorris.com.

TYNDALE and Tyndale's quill logo are registered trademarks of Tyndale House Publishers, Inc.

The Official Chuck Norris Fact Book: 101 of Chuck's Favorite Facts and Stories

Designed by Ron Kaufmann

Published in association with the literary agency of Mark Sweeney & Associates, 28540 Altessa Way, Suite 201, Bonita Springs, FL 34135.

Library of Congress Cataloging-in-Publication Data

Norris, Chuck, date.
    The official Chuck Norris fact book : 101 of Chuck's favorite facts and stories / Chuck Norris ; with Todd DuBord.
        p. cm.
    Includes bibliographical references.
    ISBN 978-1-4143-3449-3 (sc)
    1. Norris, Chuck, date. 2. Martial artists—United States—Biography. 3. Actors—United States—Biography. I. DuBord, Todd. II. Title.
    GV1113.N67N67 2009
    796.8092—dc22
    [B]   2009028695

Printed in the United States of America

15 14 13 12
14 13 12 11 10 9

For the past three years, I've been asked repeatedly to select my favorite Chuck Norris Facts. For three years, people from everywhere have inquired in person and by mail about what I think of particular Chuck Norris Facts. For three years, I've been solicited to write this manuscript. So, finally, I'm happy to offer the world *The Official Chuck Norris Fact Book*, 101 of my favorite Facts, with my personal reflections on each.

For those who have somehow not heard of the Chuck Norris Facts, they are mythical expressions of my life and abilities, a collection of sayings, quips, and quotes, created by young and old alike, that have elevated my character and personhood to almost legendary, Paul Bunyan–like dimensions.

I've heard that there are literally hundreds of thousands of Chuck Norris Facts that circle the globe. They proliferate on the Internet, are found in speeches and books, and are written on bathroom walls from schools in America to battlefields in the Middle East. (I was honored twice to visit our troops in Iraq, and I was glad to learn that the Chuck Norris Facts provide them with a daily dose of humor and encouragement.)

The Chuck Norris Facts have also reconnected me to the younger generations. To some who know little of my martial arts or film careers but perhaps grew up with *Walker, Texas Ranger*, it seems that I have become a somewhat mythical superhero icon. I am flattered and humbled.

At the same time, although I have been reintroduced to those younger generations, it has become apparent to me that they know me only in part. For example, they may know me as Walker, Texas Ranger, or maybe as a character from one of my twenty-three action films, but they don't know that I participate in humanitarian work, including nearly twenty years of promoting the **KICKSTART KIDS** program in public schools in Texas (www.kickstartkids.org); or that I've written six books besides this one; or that I write a weekly syndicated column (www.creators.com/opinion/chuck-norris.html); or that I'm engaged in America's culture wars on many fronts.

Prior to my television and movie careers, I was a martial arts champion. From 1964 to 1968, I won many state, national, and international amateur karate titles. In 1968, I fought and won the world professional middleweight karate championships by defeating the world's top fighters. I held that title until 1974, when I retired as a six-time-undefeated world professional middleweight karate champion.

In 1968, I was inducted into the Black Belt Hall of Fame as Fighter of the Year. In 1975, I was inducted as Instructor of the Year; and in 1977, I received the honor of Man of the Year. I am also founder and president of the United Fighting Arts Federation (www.ufaf.org), with more than 2,300 black belt members all over the world. My martial arts system is called Chun Kuk Do (Universal Way).

In 1997, I reached another milestone by being the first man from the Western Hemisphere ever to be awarded recognition as an eighth-degree black belt grand master in the Tae Kwon Do system. This was a first in 4,500 years of that tradition.

Because of my martial arts background and career, I was

able to become an action-movie star in more than twenty major motion pictures, followed by 203 episodes of the television series *Walker, Texas Ranger*.

FILMOGRAPHY

The Wrecking Crew (1969), starring Dean Martin
Return of the Dragon (1972), starring Bruce Lee
Breaker! Breaker! (1977)
Good Guys Wear Black (1978)
A Force of One (1979)
The Octagon (1980)
An Eye for an Eye (1981)
Silent Rage (1982)
Forced Vengeance (1982)
Lone Wolf McQuade (1983)
Missing in Action (1984)
Missing in Action 2: The Beginning (1985)
Code of Silence (1985)
Invasion U.S.A. (1985)
The Delta Force (1986)
Firewalker (1986)
Braddock: Missing in Action III (1988)
Hero and the Terror (1988)
Delta Force 2: Operation Strang}ehold (1990)
The Hitman (1991)
Sidekicks (1992)
Hellbound (1994)
Top Dog (1995)

If you didn't already know why my life experiences have been used to create the Chuck Norris Facts phenomenon, now you do. You might have heard some of the classics, but I'll bet there are many you haven't heard. The 101 Facts I've selected for this book come from all over the world—America, Europe, the Middle East, the Far East, and beyond. They're the ones I consider to be the best of the best, and they're sure to provide you with hours of laughter and encouragement.

But apart from providing a little humor break for your day, I'm also using the contents of this book to convey more about Chuck's Code, the five core values I live by, make choices by, and write about. These five principles generally summarize my life's purposes. They are represented by five *F*s: Freedom, Family, Fitness, Faith, and Fight. *Freedom*, for example, can represent anything from political to personal freedoms. *Fitness* can encompass a holistic view of mind, body, and spirit. *Fight* is not merely about the martial arts; it also includes fighting for a cause or for something you're passionate about.

For each of the Chuck Norris Facts I've chosen as my 101 favorites, I've identified the corresponding core value from Chuck's Code.

In these tough times, I think we all could use a good laugh. That's why I decided that now was the time to write this book.

I dedicate it to all Americans, and those abroad, who need a little more humor in their lives.

So happy reading! And I hope you enjoy a good CHUCKle!

Your friend,

Chuck Norris

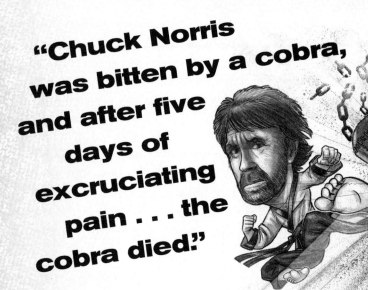

"Chuck Norris was bitten by a cobra, and after five days of excruciating pain . . . the cobra died."

LET'S BE HONEST . . .

I was filming an episode of *Walker, Texas Ranger* out in the woods. The scene was with me and a Native American actor-friend, and we were competing to see who could catch the largest rattlesnake with his bare hands.

The snake wranglers had two very large rattlesnakes, supposedly de-venomed. My friend didn't want to be filmed trying to grab the rattlesnake with his hand. So he said, "De-venomed or not, I'm not about to try it." I replied, "Why don't you just walk in from the woods holding the snake in your hand? I'm going to win anyway, because I'm grabbing the largest snake." The larger of the two rattlers was slithering on the ground, so I sneaked up from behind and grabbed it by the back of the neck, picking it up and counting the number of rattles it had.

The take went very well, but the director wanted a second take. So the snake wrangler took the snake from me and put it back on the ground. I sneaked up to grab him a second time, but just as my hand grabbed his neck, he turned and bit me on the hand! As blood started gushing out, the director panicked and took off running.

I asked the snake wrangler if he thought I should go to the hospital to see if the snake had injected venom into me. He said, "That wouldn't be a bad idea." I told the crew that we had only one take, because I had to go to the hospital and the director was missing in action! (Then I asked, "Would someone please go find him?")

There was a happy ending to it all: The single take was good, I had no venom in me, and they found the director.

Later, I played back the snakebite scene on film and slowed it down frame by frame. Twenty-four frames equal one second, and the snakebite covered three frames. In other words, that snake bit me in one-eighth of a second. Talk about fast!

THEY SAID IT . . .
"I hate snakes." > INDIANA JONES (HARRISON FORD'S CHARACTER) IN THE CLASSIC *RAIDERS OF THE LOST ARK*

CHUCK'S CODE (FIGHT)

If your opponent is fast, you must be faster or smarter.

"Chuck Norris doesn't cheat death. He defeats it fair and square."

LET'S BE HONEST . . .

As an action hero in my movies, I joined a long legacy of tough guys delivering one-liner warrior maxims. Some I still turn red saying, and others I still laugh repeating.

It's difficult to say if these hard-hitting theatrical adages created the mystique surrounding action heroes, or vice versa. In the end, however, it's the stuff that creates movie history and the classic strongman figures of entertainment folklore.

Of course, I didn't invent the tough-guy image or the tongue-in-cheek combatant quips. They existed long before I arrived on the movie and television scene. Robust, manly men have always been larger than life on stage and screen.

Here are a few of my favorite tough-guy one-liners in the movies:

"Look, you work your side of the street, and I'll work mine." (Steve McQueen in *Bullitt*, 1968)

"Out here, due process is a bullet." (John Wayne in *The Green Berets*, 1968)

"You've got to ask yourself one question: 'Do I feel lucky?' Well, do ya, punk?" (Clint Eastwood in *Dirty Harry*, 1971)

"You talkin' to me?" (Robert De Niro in *Taxi Driver*, 1976)

"He's dead tired." (Arnold Schwarzenegger, after killing a man, in *Commando*, 1985)

"I'm like a bad penny. I always turn up." (Harrison Ford in *Indiana Jones and the Last Crusade*, 1989)

"Why, Johnny Ringo, you look like somebody just walked over your grave." (Val Kilmer in *Tombstone*, 1993)

"Before this war is over, I'm going to kill you." (Mel Gibson in *The Patriot*, 2000)

Do you have a favorite tough-guy one-liner? Walk up to a friend and let it fly!

THEY SAID IT . . .
"My kind of trouble doesn't take vacations." > CHUCK NORRIS IN *LONE WOLF MCQUADE*, 1983

"When I want your opinion, I'll beat it out of you."

> CHUCK NORRIS IN *CODE OF SILENCE*, 1985

"If you come back in here, I'm going to hit you with so many rights, you're going to beg for a left." > CHUCK NORRIS IN *INVASION U.S.A.*, 1985

CHUCK'S CODE (FIGHT)

If I have nothing good to say about a person, then I will say nothing. (#6 of my Principles for Life)

"He who laughs last, laughs best. He who laughs at Chuck Norris, it's definitely his last laugh."

LET'S BE HONEST . . .

Now that's funny. I love to laugh, as do most people. But we often lack reasons to laugh, or at least it's difficult to see them, especially in tough times. Life's struggles have a way of squeezing in and squelching our humorous side. Still, I think laughter is one of the things we need most and need more of—which probably stands as the best reason for the Chuck Norris Facts proliferation.

Naturally, over the past couple of years, as this Internet wildfire has been raging about my mythical life and abilities, people everywhere have asked me, "What do you think of all this?"

My answer is always the same: Some are hilarious. Some are pretty far out. And, thankfully, most are just promoting harmless fun. (But be careful if you go searching for "Chuck Norris Facts" on the Internet, because some are just flat-out inappropriate.)

That's one of the primary reasons I wrote this book—to give people a little break in their often busy and burdened lives, and to bring a little encouragement for their life journeys.

So, as comedian Steve Allen used to say, "Don't suppress your laughter, or it will go down to your hips and spread out!"

Now we wouldn't want that to happen, would we?

THEY SAID IT . . .
"Nothing to me feels as good as laughing incredibly hard."
> COMEDIAN AND ACTOR STEVE CARELL

 CHUCK'S CODE (FITNESS)

We should be free enough from life's burdens to laugh.

OFFICIAL CHUCK
NORRIS FACT #4

"When an episode of
Walker, Texas Ranger
was aired in
France,
the French
surrendered
to Chuck
Norris, just to
be on the
safe side."

LET'S BE HONEST . . .

In 1974, while still holding the world martial arts title, I did a
tour throughout France, giving a demonstration of my ability.
I was demonstrating martial arts in cities and towns all over
France: forty-two in all. I finished each demo by jumping over

☆ **9** ☆

six volunteer spectators. They would stand side by side, slightly bent over, and I would run and jump over them, breaking five one-inch planks of wood.

During the tour, six young men decided to follow me around and be the six I would jump over. Before I could ask for volunteers to come forward out of the audience, these young men would run out first and line up next to each other.

All was going fine, except that my hosts would take me out to eat after each demo—and if you have been to Europe, you know that dinner doesn't begin until ten o'clock at night, and French food is rich and delicious. By the end of the tour, I was tired and ten pounds overweight.

The last evening of my tour, I had decided to cut my final jump down to four volunteers, mainly because the floor was concrete and I could not get any spring in my jump—along with the added pounds and exhaustion. But before I could ask for four volunteers, the six young men who were still following me ran down and lined up.

I thought to myself, *Oh man!* But before I could think much about it, I started running to make the jump. Once in the air, however, I realized I wasn't going to make it. I landed on the last man, and we crashed to the floor.

Now my adrenaline was pumping, so I picked him back up, set him back in line, and told the audience that I was going to attempt it again. This time, as I ran and jumped, my rear foot caught the back of the first man, and I flipped in the air, landing on the last man again.

Again I grabbed him, jerked him up on his feet, and put him back in line. With despair in his eyes, he asked, "Are you going to try again?" "Yes," I said as I walked back to make the run yet again. I could hear him asking one of the others in line to switch with him!

On the third try, I finally made the jump and broke the boards.

Thank goodness that was the last demo on my tour. I'm sure those young men would not have followed me to the next town—but I'm sure they still share the story.

THEY SAID IT . . .

"Success is falling nine times and getting up ten." > JON BON JOVI

 ## CHUCK'S CODE (FIGHT)

Never think to yourself, *I can't do this.* Your subconscious takes you at your word. Think positively, and your subconscious will help you succeed. Failure is not an option.

"The easiest way to determine Chuck Norris's age is to cut him in half and count the rings."

LET'S BE HONEST . . .

Three years ago, at the end of a *Nightline* interview, ABC host Bill Weir asked me my age, and I told him sixty-six. Then I added with a smile, "I like to say I'm thirty-nine with twenty-seven years of experience!"

I loved his response even more. Quoting one of the thousands of Chuck Norris Facts circulating the Internet, Bill said, "Well, according to the [Chuck Norris Facts], 'Chuck Norris doesn't age. He roundhouse kicks time in the face!'" After a huge laugh, I sincerely thought about it and replied, "That's exactly what I do!" That's exactly what I believe we all should do.

Our pastor once preached, "As far as the Bible is concerned, life begins at seventy-five." He even cited many biblical leaders who experienced their greatest fulfillment after that crest. For example, Abraham and Sarah bore a child and a nation; Moses led Israel out of captivity into the Promised Land; Joshua led military conquests in Canaan; and Simeon and Anna saw the fulfillment of the promised Messiah.

If it's true that life begins at seventy-five, I can't wait to see what God has in store for me six years from now! The way I see it, God willing, I have roughly three decades ahead to continue to serve this country and world, and I plan to make them my best and most productive. With whatever time God has blessed you on this planet, I encourage you to do the same.

THEY SAID IT . . .

"In the end, it's not the years in your life that count. It's the life in your years." > ABRAHAM LINCOLN

CHUCK'S CODE (FITNESS)

I will develop myself to the maximum of my potential
in all ways. (#1 of my Principles for Life)

"The first rule of Chuck Norris: Follow his rules or eat his roundhouse kick."

LET'S BE HONEST . . .

Rules are principles, and for almost forty years, I've done my best to live by my 12 Principles for Life. They've led me this far in life, and I know they'll lead me the rest of the way. Maybe one or two can encourage or help you.

1. I will develop myself to the maximum of my potential in all ways.
2. I will forget the mistakes of the past and press on to greater achievements.
3. I will always be in a positive frame of mind and convey this feeling to every person I meet.

4. I will continually work at developing love, happiness, and loyalty in my family and acknowledge that no other success can compensate for failure in the home.
5. I will look for the good in all people and make them feel worthwhile.
6. If I have nothing good to say about a person, then I will say nothing.
7. I will give so much time to the improvement of myself that I will have no time to criticize others.
8. I will always be as enthusiastic about the success of others as I am about my own.
9. I will maintain an attitude of open-mindedness toward another person's viewpoint, while still holding fast to that which I know to be true and honest.
10. I will maintain respect for those in authority and demonstrate this respect at all times.
11. I will always remain loyal to God, my country, family, and my friends.
12. I will remain highly goal oriented throughout my life because that positive attitude helps my family, my country, and me.

THEY SAID IT . . .

"Policies are many, principles are few—policies will change, principles never do." > JOHN C. MAXWELL

CHUCK'S CODE (FITNESS)

Never compromise your principles.

"Chuck Norris and Bruce Lee never actually fought offscreen. If they had, the universe would have imploded and we all would have been vaporized."

LET'S BE HONEST . . .

In 1972, Bruce Lee was starring in and directing *Return of the Dragon*, and he wanted me to be in it. As he was telling me about the film, he said with excitement, "I want to do a fight scene in this movie that everyone will remember. The fight will be in the Colosseum in Rome." He added, "I want you to be my opponent. It will be like two gladiators fighting in Roman times."

"Who wins?" I asked.

"I do," Bruce said with a laugh. "I'm the star!"

"Oh, I see," I said. "You want to beat up the current world karate champion!"

"No," said Bruce. "I want to *kill* the current world karate champion!"

Through the years, one of the questions I've been asked most has been, "What was it like to fight Bruce Lee?" Of course, we never actually fought offscreen, because Bruce didn't compete in professional tournaments. (He wanted to be an actor, and at the time, he was starring as Kato in the TV series *The Green Hornet*.) We did, however, work out together, and we learned each other's martial arts styles. Bruce and I became good friends, and we deeply respected each other as masters of the martial arts.

I learned a long time ago that there is no prize without perseverance. It's true on the movie screen and in the fighting ring. It's also true in the ring of life. We all know that victory comes one battle at a time. We've got to prepare for the long haul—and not expect an immediate or easy result or outcome.

Success often comes down to this one final step: Will we give up, or will we endure?

"A fight is not won by one punch or kick. Either learn to endure or hire a bodyguard." > BRUCE LEE

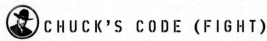

CHUCK'S CODE (FIGHT)

Anything worth achieving will always have obstacles. You've got to have that drive and determination to overcome those obstacles en route to whatever it is that you want to accomplish. A lot of people give up just before they're about to make it. You never know when that next obstacle is going to be the last one.

"When Chuck Norris was born, the only person who cried was the doctor. Never slap Chuck Norris."

LET'S BE HONEST . . .

I was born through normal delivery, if you can call seven days of labor and being born bluish-purple from prolonged oxygen deprivation normal. Mom and I both almost didn't make it. But on March 10, 1940, I weighed in for the first round of life's big fight at six pounds, eight ounces. Mom was only eighteen years old.

For the first five days of my life, the doctors and others weren't sure I was going to live. Mom still has a letter from my grandmother to my aunt, dated that same week, which says, "Wilma's baby probably isn't going to live." But we surprised them all!

The name on my birth certificate is Carlos Ray Norris. I got my first name from the Reverend Carlos Berry, my family's minister in Ryan, Oklahoma, a very small town on the border of Texas, where I was born. My middle name came from my father.

"Chuck" was actually a nickname given to me in the military. During boot camp, one of the guys in my barracks asked me about my name: "Carlos?" he said. "That's a rather odd name for someone who isn't Hispanic, isn't it? What does Carlos mean in English?" When I told him it was roughly equivalent to *Charles*, he replied, "Good, then we'll call you *Chuck*. Chuck Norris." The nickname stuck, although my family, wife, and old friends still call me Carlos.

Regarding nationality, I'm equal parts Irish and Indian. My paternal grandfather was Irish, and my grandmother was a full-blooded Cherokee. On my mother's side, my grandfather was a Cherokee from Kentucky, and my grandmother, Granny Scarberry, was Irish.

Life has been a fight for me right from the beginning. When Mom was finally able to hold me in her arms, she looked into my eyes and said, "God has big plans for you." It is a message she has said repeatedly through my life. And whether you believe it or not, I believe it's true for your life as well.

THEY SAID IT . . .

"'Diaper' backward spells 'repaid.' Think about it."

> MARSHALL MCLUHAN

CHUCK'S CODE (FAMILY)

I will continually work at developing love, happiness, and loyalty in my family and acknowledge that no other success can compensate for failure in the home. (#4 of my Principles for Life)

OFFICIAL CHUCK NORRIS FACT #9

"On Valentine's Day, Chuck Norris gives his wife the still-beating heart of one of his enemies."

(Being the romantic type, Chuck believes every day should be Valentine's Day.)

LET'S BE HONEST . . .

I met my true valentine, my wife Gena, when I was filming *Walker, Texas Ranger*. One of my best friends, Larry Morales, came to Dallas for a visit while I was filming. At the time, I was living the single life, and even though I had a successful TV series, I was still miserable. Larry realized that I had everything but I had nothing, so he decided to introduce me to a lady he wanted me to meet. It just so happened that she had a modeling assignment in Dallas.

One evening, I was at a sushi restaurant with about twelve people, including a date, when Larry walked in with a young lady. He began introducing her to everyone, but I was engrossed in conversation with my date and didn't notice—that is, until Larry called my name and said he wanted me to meet Gena. I looked up at her, and all I could see was an angel staring into my eyes. I stuttered, "Oh . . . er . . . hi! Nice to meet you."

When I finally turned back to my date, all I could see were daggers in her eyes. She immediately got up and left.

After the meal, Larry took Gena back to her hotel. But the next morning she and I had breakfast together, and she invited me to her fashion show, where she was modeling wedding gowns. One particular gown had a long train, and as Gena was walking, it hooked on a potted plant, and she dragged it down the runway. She was quite embarrassed.

Kiddingly, I said, "I was thinking about buying that potted plant."

The next day, I called my mom and told her all about Gena and about her modeling gowns. Mom said, "Is that giving you any ideas about marriage?"

"Nope," I said. "I'm never getting married again."

Famous last words! We've now been married more than ten years and have eight-year-old twins. I should also mention that Gena is my best friend, the love of my life, and the instrument to my spiritual renewal.

It's easy to get caught up in infatuation, but true love takes time and a lot of work. If you're dating, you must not leave your brains at the door.

Don't merely consider the other person's outer traits, but discover what makes that person tick on the inside—especially spiritually. Don't compromise your morals or principles when dating or searching for a soul mate. Make sure your core values and beliefs align with the other person's.

And don't be in a rush—take your time. Otherwise, you might succumb to the folly of Socrates, who once said, "By all means marry. If you get a good wife, you'll become happy. If you get a bad one, you'll become a philosopher."

THEY SAID IT . . .

"She is but half a wife who is not a friend." > WILLIAM PENN, FOUNDER OF PENNSYLVANIA

CHUCK'S CODE (FAMILY)

Fireproof your marriage: watch the movie *Fireproof*, starring Kirk Cameron.

"Even Google can't find Chuck Norris."

LET'S BE HONEST . . .

Some months ago, Arran Schlosberg, an Australian Web developer, produced a fun, fake Google-type search Web page with me at the heart of it: www.NoChuckNorris.com. As *WorldNetDaily* noted, "It may be the ultimate Chuck Norris joke for people who like to pass along funny items or peculiarities to their e-mail lists."[1]

The site mimics an ordinary Google search page with the term "Chuck Norris" already inserted in the search bar. But the search results say, "Google won't search for Chuck Norris because it knows you don't find Chuck Norris, he finds you." It also offers the following two suggestions: (1) "Run, before he finds you" and (2) "Try a different person."

As Mr. Schlosberg explained to *WorldNetDaily*, "The goal of this site is to have the top Google ranking with the keywords 'Chuck Norris,' so that when these are searched for using the 'I'm Feeling Lucky' function, this page will appear."[2]

We live in a postmodern world in which computers and the Internet have become an integral part of all we do. They are used for everything under the sun, from purchasing to investing, from downloading to burning, and from dating to providing the platform for one's primary social network.

According to a new Harris poll, just under half of all Americans (48 percent) use Twitter or have a MySpace or Facebook page. Seventy-four percent of eighteen- to thirty-four-year-olds, and even 24 percent of those fifty-five and older, have an account on Facebook or MySpace. Eight percent of those eighteen to thirty-four years old use Twitter, as do 7 percent of thirty-five- to forty-four-year-olds, 4 percent of those forty-five to fifty-four, and 1 percent of those fifty-five and older.

Another Harris poll shows that one in ten children and teens (three million kids) who play video games show behavioral signs that may indicate addiction. The study found that 8.5 percent of those who played video games exhibited at least six of eleven addictive symptoms, including avoiding chores and homework and playing games to escape problems. Other symptoms include excessive thinking and planning about games when not playing, lying about playing, trying to play less and failing, being restless or irritable when trying to reduce or stop playing, stealing a game, or stealing money to buy a game.[3]

That is why I offer one final encouragement and caution in this entry: Be careful that computers don't control your life; make sure that you control them (as well as your other electronic media). They should be an aid to you, not an albatross around your neck.

THEY SAID IT . . .

"'Everything is permissible'—but not everything is beneficial. 'Everything is permissible'—but not everything is constructive."

> 1 CORINTHIANS 10:23, NIV

CHUCK'S CODE (FIGHT)

Don't be obsessed. Be disciplined. Enjoy people and things, but not to the point of addiction.

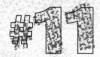

"On the seventh day, God rested . . . and Chuck Norris took over."

LET'S BE HONEST . . .

Now there's a serious exaggeration! God obviously did just fine without me there at creation. If I had taken over after the six days of creation, odds are we wouldn't have made it through one-seventh of the seventh day. And all we had to do was rest!

Creation is simply amazing and awe inspiring. Whether one considers a single-cell amoeba, a stellar explosion, or anything in between, it's difficult not to marvel at every corner of the pristine exquisiteness of creation. When was the last time you looked closely at a raindrop, a leaf, or the human eye? I'll admit that I don't know exactly why or how everything fits together, like the platypus or pesky mosquitoes, but everything seems to have its purpose.

Creation is the greatest playground, and this may be the most awesome thing of all: We have five senses in order to experience it. It would be enough that butterflies and mountain cascades existed, but to be there for our enjoyment is a supreme cherry on the creation sundae.

You might believe that creation rolled off some naturalistic assembly line, but I join the billions of others who clearly see the fingerprints of a Great Designer behind it all.[1] Despite what one believes about evolution, it can't and doesn't disprove a Creator.[2]

As Paul Davies, the renowned British-born physicist, agnostic, and professor of cosmology, quantum field theory, and astrobiology, once said, "If you admit that we can't peer behind a curtain, how can you be sure there's nothing there?"[3]

The Bible summarizes it well: "For since the creation of the world [God's] invisible attributes—his eternal power and divine nature—have been understood and observed by what he made, so that people are without excuse."[4]

THEY SAID IT . . .

"To this may be truly added, that serious religion, under its various denominations, is not only tolerated, but respected and practiced. Atheism is unknown there." > BENJAMIN FRANKLIN, IN HIS 1782 PAMPHLET FOR EUROPEANS THINKING OF RELOCATING TO AMERICA

CHUCK'S CODE (FAITH)

I will always remain loyal to God, my country, my family, and my friends. (#11 of my Principles for Life)

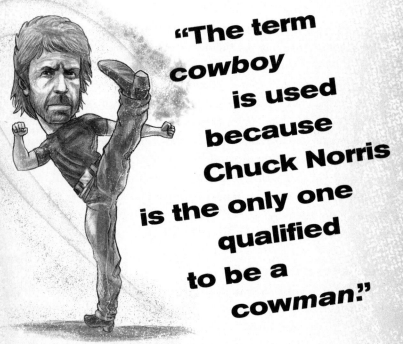

"The term cowboy is used because Chuck Norris is the only one qualified to be a cowman."

LET'S BE HONEST . . .

While I was in Israel filming the movie *Hellbound* in 1992, my manager called and asked if I would be interested in doing a weekly TV series with CBS called *Walker, Texas Ranger*, a modern-day story of a Texas Ranger with old-fashioned values who champions right over wrong. At first, I was reluctant, but when he told me that the series would be about a cowboy-type law officer fighting crime in a modern Texas city, it piqued my interest.

The thought of playing a Texas Ranger intrigued me. When I was growing up, my favorite movies were Westerns. Their overriding message was the Code of the West—friendship, loyalty, and integrity—values I felt ought to be reflected in a television series. I decided to take the risk of jumping from movies to television.

I believe that people want and need heroes. Many people, especially young people, want someone with whom they can identify, a man or a woman who is self-reliant, stands on his or her own two feet, and is not afraid to face adversity. I decided that if I was going to do a series, this should be the one. My personal beliefs became the core traits of Cordell Walker, the lead character in the television series.

It sounds kind of canned, but I truly believe that there is a hero in all of us. Everyone was designed by God to be a blessing to others—a champion to someone. In our society today, we need champions more than ever. We need heroes. And don't think you can't be that hero. You might not be called upon to save someone's life, but all of us can make a difference in someone's life through acts of kindness, mercy, and modeling a life of decency and integrity.

THEY SAID IT . . .
"It's not their abilities that make them heroes. It's their choices."
> FROM *HEROES*, THE TELEVISION SERIES

 CHUCK'S CODE (FIGHT)

I truly believe that there is a hero in all of us. Everyone was designed by God to be a blessing to others—a champion to someone.

OFFICIAL CHUCK
NORRIS FACT

"When
Chuck Norris
wants an egg,
he cracks open
a chicken."

LET'S BE HONEST . . .

Speaking of *chicken*, some people might find it interesting to know that I used to be afraid to speak in public.

I left Korea in 1961 as a black belt in Tang Soo Do (karate) and a brown belt in judo and was stationed at March Air Force Base in Riverside, California. When I practiced my martial arts at the base gym, others would watch and many would ask me to teach them.

I decided to give a demonstration on the base to see how much interest there would be in starting a martial arts club. I circulated flyers around the base, advertising the demonstration.

Then I realized I would have to give a talk prior to the demonstration. I was twenty-one years old and had never spoken in front of a crowd, so I wrote out a half-page speech and memorized it for two weeks. I could say it forward and backward.

The night of the demonstration, there were about four hundred people gathered in the auditorium. As I walked in dressed in my karate *gi* and saw all the people there, I immediately began sweating with fear.

I can still remember that feeling like it was yesterday. I walked over to where the microphone was lying on the floor, picked it up, and said, "Good evening, ladies and gentlemen. My name is Chuck Norris, and I would like to welcome you here . . ."

That's the last thing I remember until I was walking out into the middle of the auditorium to do my demonstration. As I was walking, I thought to myself, *Did I finish my speech, or did I just lay the microphone down?*

To this day, I still don't know. But the important point is that I finally cracked the egg of insecurity I had lived in for twenty-one years. Eventually, that egg cracked wide open.

"Not for the sake of glory, not for the sake of fame, not for the sake of success, but for the sake of my soul." > RACHEL JOY SCOTT, FIRST VICTIM OF THE COLUMBINE SHOOTINGS[1]

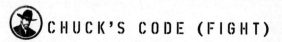 **CHUCK'S CODE (FIGHT)**

Face your fears and conquer them. If you do something you have previously been afraid to do, you will begin to crack the egg of your insecurity. Accomplishing something difficult gives you the strength to go on to further success.

"Why were no weapons of mass destruction found in the Middle East? Because Chuck Norris lives in Texas."

LET'S BE HONEST . . .

War is never easy, and it can often be controversial. Indeed, as General Sherman said, "War is hell." Still, despite our divergent views on warfare, we all can agree that our servicemen and servicewomen deserve our support and commendation. I am humbled by their courage and grateful for their service.

Thanking our military is why, in 2006 and 2007, I visited our troops in the Middle East. I went to twenty-eight bases and shook hands with nearly forty thousand troops. It was an experience I will remember for the rest of my life.

When I first arrived in Iraq, some of the troops held up a huge sign that said, "Chuck Norris is here! We can go home now!" I wish that were true.

Even in the severity of war, I was pleased to see that our troops could enjoy lighter moments, even using my name and reputation. I still smile when I think about the Special Forces unit that had named their vehicle after me. Other units not only adopted my image on their vehicles, but one even had the call sign of "Walker."

While I was overseas, one soldier said that the only way he would reenlist was if the unit "got Chuck Norris out here." I was told about this while I was visiting the base where he was stationed. When I met him, the soldier asked me to put him into an arm bar (twisting his arm) as he happily signed his reenlistment paperwork. (I'm a patriot, so what else could I do but oblige?)

I'll be honest with you. I understand why people are against the wars we're in. But I simply don't understand how anyone could neglect to support these fine servicemen and servicewomen. It is not only unpatriotic; it's unjust.

The military is very close to my heart because it turned my life around. Joining the Air Force helped me get on the right path.

I still believe it can help others, too. That is why I stand with the majority of Americans who say to all our service members, their families, and indeed all the veterans who have served this great country and the cause of freedom, "We salute you. We support you. And we will continue to pray for you."

THEY SAID IT . . .
"It doesn't take a hero to order men into battle. It takes a hero to be one of those men who goes into battle." > GENERAL NORMAN SCHWARZKOPF

 # CHUCK'S CODE (FREEDOM)

Think of yourself as a leader rather than a follower. Your subconscious mind will take it as a fact, and you will act accordingly.

OFFICIAL CHUCK
NORRIS FACT #15

"Superman wears Chuck Norris pajamas to bed at night."

LET'S BE HONEST . . .

Whenever I think of pajamas, I can't help but reflect on one of the most hilarious and possibly embarrassing "lower-garment moments" of my life and career, and it happened with my good friend, martial arts pupil, and great actor of yesteryear Steve McQueen.

Steve was a good student and a tough guy, but his biggest challenge was his lack of flexibility. He was not very limber and had difficulty executing high kicks. So Ali McGraw, Steve's wife, invited Steve and me to join her at her stretching class in Beverly Hills.

When Steve and I arrived, Shirley Jones and Susan Dey, stars of the classic TV show *The Partridge Family*, were already there. The class

☆ **39** ☆

instructor immediately held out a pair of flimsy, skintight leotards for us to put on. One pair was pink, and the other was blue. I grabbed the blue pair. We went into the locker room to change. To say we looked ridiculous in those outfits would be an understatement.

Steve said, "I'm not going out there looking like this!"

"Listen, Steve," I said, "Let's just walk out there and act like we've been doing this for years. No one will even notice."

"Okay," he said reluctantly. He walked out of the dressing room in his pink leotard.

As soon as he stepped out the door, I shut it and locked it. Steve pounded on the door, with a few choice words for me, but I didn't unlock it. I figured that after the girls got tired of looking and laughing at him, they wouldn't pay any attention to me.

Sure enough, I heard everyone laughing. After the laughter subsided, I walked out of the dressing room and saw Steve in the studio, sitting on the floor and talking to the women. I casually walked over and sat down next to him. I was right! The only one who even looked at me was Steve—and if looks could kill, I would have been dead.

THEY SAID IT . . .

"In my own mind, I'm not sure that acting is something for a grown man to be doing." > STEVE MCQUEEN

CHUCK'S CODE (FITNESS)

Count the cost before doing anything—the
greatest price may not be monetary.

"Chuck Norris never uses a stunt double, except during crying scenes."

LET'S BE HONEST . . .

I can't say I *never* used a stunt double, but I did try to do most of my own stunts in my movies. One particular stunt, in *Missing in Action*, turned out to be a little more dangerous than I had bargained for.

In the scene, I rescued several POWs from a Vietnamese prison camp, and we headed to the coast, where a helicopter was to fly in and pick us up. We were out in the ocean, in water up to our necks, as the chopper hovered overhead. I started helping the POWs climb up the ladder, one by one.

As the helicopter loaded the last POW, the pilot was supposed to lift me a few feet out of the water as I hung onto the ladder and the cameramen finished the shot. It was supposed to be only a few feet because the wind was blowing so hard that the stunt coordinator was afraid I might be blown so high to the sides that I would hit the rotor blades.

As I was being pulled up out of the water, hanging onto the bottom slat of the ladder and expecting only to be lifted up a couple of feet, the helicopter took off and headed out to sea. There I was—with no safety harness—hanging on for dear life.

As the helicopter reached about three hundred feet of altitude, I was looking down at the water and wondering, *If I let go, will the drop kill me?*

The crew was finally able to contact the pilot, and he returned to the beach and dropped me off. But they had to pry my hands off the ladder!

I later asked the stunt coordinator, "If I had decided to drop into the water, would it have killed me?"

"Deader than a doornail," he replied.

THEY SAID IT . . .

"When you come to the end of your rope, tie a knot and hang on."
> FRANKLIN D. ROOSEVELT

🕵 CHUCK'S CODE (FIGHT)

If you let go, you'll never know what might have been.
Hang on—perseverance will win the day and bring you victory.

"Chuck Norris lost both his legs in a car accident but was still able to walk it off."

LET'S BE HONEST . . .

Like some of the Chuck Norris Facts, this one might be regarded as distasteful, especially to those who have suffered because of the loss of limbs. But I wish to view the Fact as many have come to view disabilities: as a detour to a meaningful life.

Bob Wieland was in his third year at the University of Wisconsin, heading toward a baseball career with the Philadelphia Phillies, when Uncle Sam extended an invitation for him to serve in Vietnam as a combat medic.

In June 1969, as he ran to help a buddy who had stepped on a booby-trapped field of mortar rounds, Bob stepped on one designed to destroy tanks. Everyone thought Bob was dead, but he miraculously survived, despite losing both of his legs.

As Bob sat in agonizing recovery for months, he contemplated his personal losses, which included his future in baseball, and a life without the ability to walk. He faced a future filled with absolute uncertainty and a host of obstacles.

Most people would become chronically depressed and even bitter. But Bob chose to face his legless life with courage, hope, and faith. He also found purpose in his pain. As Bob has said, "My legs went one way, and my life went another."

Bob began to lift weights, even while he was still in a hospital bed, and eventually became a four-time world-record holder in the bench press. He has completed several marathons and the Ford Ironman World Championship triathlon in Kona, Hawaii. He has crossed the country twice on a 6,200-mile bike circuit but is best known for his walk across America, which he completed on his hands in just over three and a half years.

Bob's life epitomizes the principles of perseverance, optimism, and belief for a better day. He's a shining example of how to overcome adversity and suffering, and that one's life, though radically altered, can still have purpose and fulfillment. He is known as "Mr. Inspiration" among motivational speakers and has been honored with many awards and achievements through the years from military and civilian organizations.

I've thought of Bob Wieland many times as I've visited our wounded warriors at Walter Reed Army Medical Center and other hospitals around the world. As tough as the road to recovery is for many of our veterans, I believe Bob's life can inspire them to still have a meaningful life. I highly recommend his story and book, *One Step at a Time: The Remarkable True Story of Bob Wieland.*

THEY SAID IT . . .

"Every time I look in a mirror, put on my hair, stick on my ear, and start my day . . . forgetting is not possible. Forgiving is."

> DAVE ROEVER, ANOTHER WOUNDED WARRIOR MAKING A BIG DIFFERENCE[1]

CHUCK'S CODE (FREEDOM)

Be grateful for those who secure your freedom. Thank a vet.

"Chuck Norris does not get frostbite. Chuck Norris bites frost."

LET'S BE HONEST . . .

After Mr. Shin, my instructor in Korea, told me I was ready to test for my black belt, he and several other Korean black belts drilled me over and over on the various techniques I had already practiced to exhaustion hundreds of times before. By the time I was scheduled to face the board of examiners in Seoul, I was very confident.

It was the dead of winter and freezing outside. The roads were icy, and it took two hours to drive there in my military truck. The *dojang* (training hall) was a big, unheated building with wind blowing through the paneless windows. It was freezing inside. I changed into my *gi* (uniform) and sat down cross legged on the bare wooden floor, along with about two hundred other students from Seoul and villages across Korea who were also testing. I was the only student from Osan Air Base. The board of examiners sat stone-faced at the table.

The testing began with one student at a time stepping forward to perform a *kata*, a combination of positions and movements, before the board. After I had been sitting cold and stiff for about three hours, my name was called. I uncrossed my legs and stood up, a bit wobbly from having sat for so long. I walked over and stood in front of the examiners and bowed.

They told me to do the form called *bassai*. I had done *bassai* countless times, but for the life of me, I could not remember how to do it. I must have had a brain freeze from the cold and my nervousness. The examiners realized I didn't know it and told me to sit down. I had failed my first attempt at earning my black belt.

Mr. Shin said nothing about my failing the test. It was almost as if the exam had never happened. He didn't scold me or belittle me for my mental lapse. He told me to put it behind me and be prepared next time, which I did. I trained harder than ever, determined not to fail again. I tested again four months later and passed with flying colors.

"In the process of trial and error, our failed attempts are meant to destroy arrogance and provoke humility." > MASTER JIN KWON, SOUTH KOREAN MARTIAL ARTS MASTER

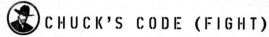

CHUCK'S CODE (FIGHT)

Failures are but stepping-stones on the path to success.

OFFICIAL CHUCK
NORRIS FACT #19

"When the boogeyman goes to sleep at night, he checks his closet for Chuck Norris."

LET'S BE HONEST . . .

My eight-year-old twins, Dakota and Danilee, have never really worried about the boogeyman with me around. Actually, the sign on our front door probably helps too. It has a picture of a gun and the words, "We don't dial 9-1-1 here."

☆ **49** ☆

One of my **KICKSTART KIDS** instructors is teaching the twins the martial arts. They are purple belts at the present time. In April of 2009, I entered them in their first karate tournament. As a proud father, I'd like to announce that Danilee took first place in sparring and forms. Dakota took third place in sparring and forms.

Watching Dakota and Danilee brings me back to the days when my oldest boys, Mike and Eric, now forty-six and forty-three respectively, were training in the martial arts. They also won a few tournaments, but other sports took over before they could earn their black belts. I'm hoping Dakota and Danilee will continue on to black belt.

The one thing I appreciate about all seven of my kids is that they're not embarrassed to show affection. They'll even give me a kiss anytime, anywhere, and in front of anyone. I appreciate that more than words can say.

One of my favorite memories happened one day when I drove then-ten-year-old Eric to school. When I pulled up in front of the school, four of his friends were standing there waiting for him. As I stopped, he leaned over and gave me a kiss before getting out of the car.

As he got out and approached the boys, one of them made a crack, laughing, "Do you still kiss your dad?"

Eric grabbed him by the shirt, pulled him up close to his face, and said, "Yeah, what of it?"

The boy immediately stopped laughing and said, "Oh nothing," and they all walked off.

I witnessed the incident and was so proud of my son I could hardly contain myself.

"Tell him he's Wayne Gretzky." > TED GREEN, COACH OF THE
EDMONTON OILERS, WHEN CENTER SHAUN VAN ALLEN SUFFERED
A CONCUSSION AND DIDN'T KNOW WHO HE WAS

CHUCK'S CODE (FAMILY)

Believe in your kids and treat them as if they
can excel further than you can or have.

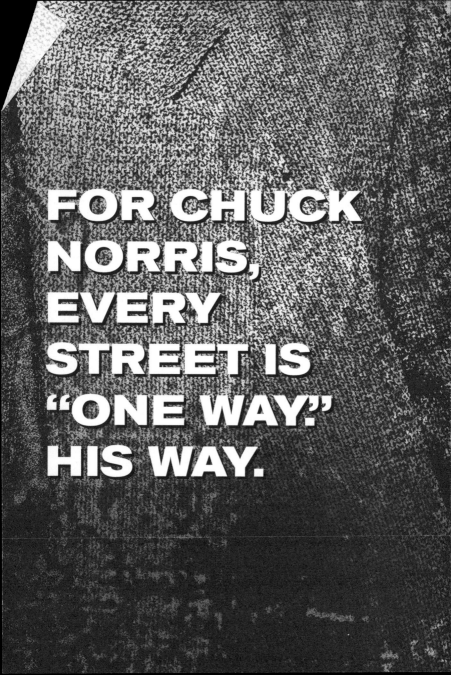

FOR CHUCK
NORRIS,
EVERY
STREET IS
"ONE WAY."
HIS WAY.

"When the going gets tough, the tough get Chuck Norris."

LET'S BE HONEST . . .

I was invited to fly out to sea with a "Top Gun" pilot and land on the aircraft carrier USS *Nimitz*. When I arrived at the Marine Corps Air Station at Miramar, just north of San Diego, I was informed by a training commander that because I was flying out to sea, I would have to undergo two days of survival training.

The first undertaking was water survival. I had to put on a flight suit, along with a pair of boots that weighed a couple of pounds each. I was then placed at the edge of a pool that was ten feet deep—and the longest one I had ever seen. I looked at the other end and thought, *I don't know if I could make it across even without all this gear on.*

As I was in the middle of my thought, they shoved me in. I started swimming for all I was worth and barely made it to the other end of the pool. As I was trying to catch my breath, I heard someone shout, "Now swim back!"

I started swimming back, but about halfway I was so tired I stopped kicking my feet and sank to the bottom of the pool. Thinking someone would be on the surface to get me, I kicked up to the surface, but no one was around. So I sank back down to the bottom of the pool. Again I kicked up to the surface—still, no one was around. So I sank a third time and kicked up again—still no one. On my fourth trip up to the surface, they pushed a little life raft out for me. With my last ounce of strength, I climbed into the raft.

The second undertaking was an altitude chamber. There were six of us in the chamber, and we paired up. My partner was an admiral. Our first instructions were to start playing patty-cake with our partners. As the oxygen became thinner, we slowly were unable to focus or control our movements—our hands clapped air rather than each other.

As the admiral and I left the chamber, I told him about my water-survival experience. He said, "You didn't have to do that. They just wanted to see what you were made of."

I said, "Well, they got a firsthand look!"

The next day, we flew 240 miles out to sea to meet up with the

USS *Nimitz*. My Top Gun pilot's call name was "Maverick." He did three touch-and-goes before finally landing the F-14 Tomcat. I was then given a tour of the carrier and was able to meet and shake hands with all the sailors and marines.

As we were flying back to Miramar, Maverick said to me, "Let's pretend there's a bogey on our tail." He immediately went into evasive maneuvers, spinning one way and then the other, hitting up to seven Gs!

After about ten minutes of that, I was about ready to hurl, but I thought, *If I do, he will tell all his Top Gun buddies.* So I said to Maverick in my headset, "Maverick, we lost him!"

Maverick laughed and said, "I know what you mean."

THEY SAID IT . . .

"We are not retreating—we are advancing in another direction."

> GENERAL DOUGLAS MACARTHUR

 CHUCK'S CODE (FREEDOM)

You can't sit back and wait for breaks to come your way. They don't happen by hoping; they happen because of positive actions. Maintain a positive attitude about anything you want to achieve, and do what has to be done.

"The real, full name of the UFC is Ultimate Fighting Championship: Non–Chuck Norris Division."

LET'S BE HONEST . . .

This entry is for all the mixed martial arts enthusiasts out there who are fans of the UFC, WCL, or other combat sports, as I am.

In 1982, I was in Rio de Janeiro, Brazil, on a scuba-diving trip. While I was there, I visited various martial arts schools in Rio and worked out with the students and instructors. All I heard about in these schools was Gracie Jiu-Jitsu and how no one would dare mess with its students. That piqued my interest, and I was determined to track down their school, which eventually I was able to do.

When I walked in to meet Helio Gracie, the founder of Gracie Jiu-Jitsu, several of his sons were working out, and they invited me to work out with them.

I first worked out with Royce Gracie. (Fans of MMA know that Royce dominated the UFC for several years.) Then I worked out with Rickson Gracie, who at the time was the best jujitsu fighter in the world. Finally I worked out with the master himself, Mr. Helio Gracie.

He was in his early seventies and still tough as nails. As Mr. Gracie and I grappled, I was able to mount him—which is a martial arts term for getting on top of your opponent. Mr. Gracie then told me to punch him in the face. Startled, I said, "I can't do that, Mr. Gracie." He insisted. So I drew my hand back timidly, like I was going to strike. That's the last thing I remember. When I woke up a few moments later, Mr. Gracie apologized profusely for choking me so hard. I said that was fine, even though I could hardly swallow for a couple of days!

I trained with the whole family until I had to leave to start filming *Lone Wolf McQuade*. Mr. Gracie asked me to stay and train with the family and said he would make me an incredible jujitsu practitioner. I was tempted to stay, but I was just starting to get my movie career going, so I had to decline. However, I did continue training in Los Angeles with the Machado brothers, who are cousins of the Gracies.

Helio Gracie recently passed away at the age of ninety-five. The world has lost the best of the best.

THEY SAID IT . . .

"The Jiu-Jitsu that I created was designed to give the weak ones a chance to face the heavy and strong. It was so successful that they decided to create a sportive version of it. I would like to make it clear that, of course, I am in favor of the sportive practice and technical refinement of all athletes, whatever their specialty may be, as well as good nutrition, sexual control, avoidance of addictions, and unhealthy habits." > HELIO GRACIE

CHUCK'S CODE (FIGHT)

Respect your elders—or they might help you!

"Chuck Norris was born in a log cabin that he built with his bare hands."

LET'S BE HONEST . . .

We moved thirteen times before I was fifteen years old. A few months after I was born, Granny Scarberry, my mother's mother and a widow with two daughters still at home, needed my parents' help. So we moved into her very small house in Wilson, Oklahoma. My dad, who was a mechanic, got a job with a car dealership in town. When Granny was better, we moved to Lawton, Oklahoma, where Dad drove a Greyhound bus.

When World War II came, Dad had the choice of being drafted or working for a defense plant. His brother lived in Richmond, California, so he went there and worked for a shipyard. Without Dad around, we moved back into Granny's house in Wilson, while my mother was pregnant with my brother Wieland. Near the end of the pregnancy, Dad came back and moved us out to Richmond, where Wieland was born. Afterward, my dad was drafted into the Army and went abroad to fight, so we went back yet again to Granny's house in Oklahoma.

Until Mom divorced Dad, we hopped, skipped, and jumped around the country, living here and there, never having any roots. But I believe Mom would have stayed with Dad even through his philandering with other women if he would have at least worked and supported his family. We lived on welfare for more than ten years. All that moving had an effect on me. Once I started to earn a living, I wanted to settle down. But it was not always easy for me to do. I still feel unsettled sometimes. Ever notice it's much easier to settle *on* a home than *in* one? I've often found myself praying that African proverb, "Lord, help my heart to sit down." It really is important to learn to bloom where you're planted.

> "I can see it inside
> It's my heart that sees, not my eyes
> And if you listen close I'll tell you why
> Home is where the heart is
> And my heart is at home with you."

> LYNYRD SKYNYRD, "HOME IS WHERE THE HEART IS"[1]

 # CHUCK'S CODE (FAMILY)

Bloom where you're planted. Pray,
"Lord, help my heart to sit down."

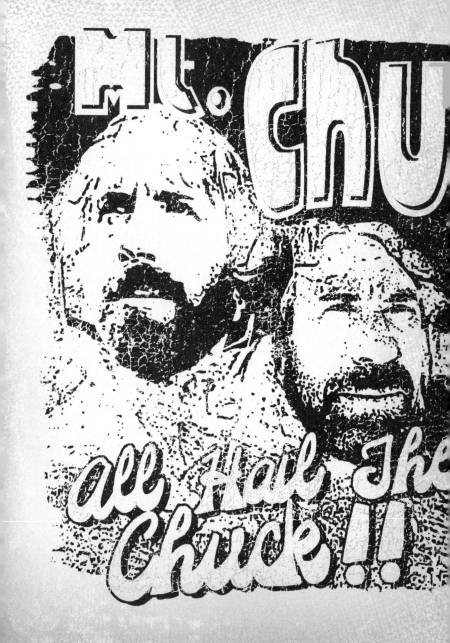

"There is no chin behind Chuck Norris's beard. There is only another fist."

LET'S BE HONEST . . .

In August 1962, right after I was discharged from the Air Force, my brother Wieland and I decided to drive to Wilson, Oklahoma, to visit with our granny.

It was late one evening, and we were driving out in the middle of nowhere in the Arizona desert when Wieland said he had to go to the bathroom. We came across a lone little gas station, only to find that the men's bathroom was out of order. The women's restroom worked, but there was no lock on the door. Exchanging looks, I said to Wieland, "I will stand outside the door while you do your duty. Then, after you're finished, you guard the door for me."

Everything went as planned until it was my turn in the bathroom. Instead of watching the door, Wieland decided to go talk to the gas station attendant. Just then, a vehicle pulled up, and a lady got out and headed for the women's bathroom. Guess what my brother did? Nothing!

She opened the bathroom door, and there I was sitting on the commode! She stared at me and I stared at her for what seemed like an eternity. Finally, I said, "Excuse me!"

She slammed the door and stomped back to her car. I could hear her yelling, "Doesn't he know that's the women's bathroom?"

When I came out, Wieland and the attendant were busting a gut laughing. I said, "Wieland, one of these days I am going to get you back!"

A few months later, I got my chance. Wieland and I had just finished a martial arts workout, and we were soaking wet with sweat. Because we were also sore from the workout, we decided to go get a massage. Unbeknownst to Wieland, I took my soaking wet underwear with me. Then, when Wieland went in for his massage, I switched his dry pair of underwear with the wet ones I had brought in.

After Wieland's massage was finished, the massage therapist went to get his clothes for him and picked up the soaking wet underwear. She was horrified as she handed him his clothes and the wet underwear. Wieland began stuttering, beet-red with embarrassment, saying that it wasn't his underwear.

"Whatever," the massage therapist replied.

As I watched the events unfold, remembering my own embarrassing moment in the gas station bathroom, I laughed hysterically as Wieland attempted to explain the situation. But the more he tried to explain that I had been the one to put the wet underwear with his clothes, the worse it got. Finally, he gave up.

After we had left the massage facility, Wieland stormed up to me and said, "Carlos, that was really a rotten thing to do."

As we walked to the car with my arm around his shoulder, I replied, "Paybacks are a bugger, little brother."

THEY SAID IT . . .

"The Statue of Liberty is no longer holding a torch and saying, 'Give me your poor, your tired, your huddled masses.' She's got a baseball bat and she's yelling, 'You want a piece of me?'"
> ROBIN WILLIAMS

CHUCK'S CODE (FAMILY)

Always make sure you post a guard you can trust outside your door.

"As President Roosevelt said, 'We have nothing to fear but fear itself.' And fear has nothing to fear but Chuck Norris."

LET'S BE HONEST . . .

Fears are funny things. As children, we grow up being afraid of the dark or of being alone. In our teenage years, we try to convince everyone that we're afraid of nothing at all. Then, as adults, it gets a little trickier. Outwardly we're okay with saying we're afraid of things such as heights, flying, or speed. But we suppress the bigger—and weightier—fears of life: fear of failure, fear of commitment, fear of letting go, fear of getting old, fear of dying, etc.

I don't believe fears are bad in themselves, but only when we allow them to rule our lives. We need to confront our fears—repeatedly, if even by baby steps, until we are released from their grip. Fear is the acknowledged absence of God; it is the polar opposite of trust.

It took me too long to realize that fear of failure isn't bad—but not stepping out in faith is. Someone once told me, "If you've never stubbed your toe, you're probably standing still."

Even the best fail, but the difference is their attitude about failure. They're not afraid to fail, and to do so over and over again. As Robert F. Kennedy once said, "Only those who dare to fail greatly can ever achieve greatly."

Remember Thomas Edison, who after failing to create a lightbulb nearly ten thousand times, said, "I have not failed. I've just found ten thousand ways that won't work."

The way I see it, too many people have near-life experiences. Always bunting, but never knowing the thrill of hitting a home run. And why? Because they're always afraid they're going to strike out.

THEY SAID IT . . .

> *"But the voice of truth tells me a different story.*
> *The voice of truth says 'Do not be afraid!'"*

> CASTING CROWNS, "VOICE OF TRUTH"

CHUCK'S CODE (FIGHT)

Do not fear fear. It is only **F**alse **E**vidence **A**ppearing **R**eal.

"Chuck Norris's mind is connected to the Internet. He refreshes Web pages by blinking."

LET'S BE HONEST . . .

I'm still amazed by the power of the Internet. The whole New Media revolution is still a bit overwhelming. Wikipedia defines *New Media* as "a term describing media that can only be created or used with the aid of computer processing power. It is a form of media that includes some aspect of interactivity for its audience and is usually in digital form."

It seems like only a few years ago when computers were huge electronic monstrosities reserved only for a few in the back rooms of America's futuristic businesses. Now most of us do absolutely everything via the Internet, on our laptops, cell phones, or BlackBerries. We communicate with friends, relatives, and coworkers; watch our favorite shows or videos; get our news, weather, and directions; conduct commerce, get a date, and shop.

To speak of watching the evening news with the late Walter Cronkite or Peter Jennings seems like reminiscing about archaic forms of reporting. A recent article in *Forbes* noted, "As such, the media model as we know it is on its way out."[1]

My own persona has been utterly transformed by the power of the Internet, through which the Chuck Norris Facts proliferation has elevated my movie and television tough-guy image to a mythic superhero legend.

The truth is that the Internet is a huge blessing, but it can also be a huge curse.

On the positive side, we can use the Internet for e-mailing, instant messaging, Skyping a friend or relative, or ordering music or a host of other things. On the negative side, there is everything from online gambling to pornography to sexual predators that prey upon hearts and minds.

That's why FBI agent Arnold Bell said, "The Internet is a great place, but there are certain parts of town you don't want to be."[2]

So do you practice safe surfing? If so, you should be able to answer *yes* to the following questions:

1. Do you seek computer counsel from experts who seek to empower young people to make wise online choices? For example, check out the Web Wise Kids Web site (webwisekids. org). They have lots of great advice.
2. Do you have an accountability friend or partner, one with whom you can share your passwords and whom you've given permission to ask and review what you're doing online?
3. Are your electronic media protected by anti-porn software? The best of these software programs can filter peer-to-peer communications, e-mails, instant messages, and chat room exchanges.
4. Lastly, are you willing to report obscene or criminal online activity? If you suspect illegal or even shady behavior from someone online, inform others—your parents, friends, and even law enforcement. Information submitted to www.ObscenityCrimes.org is forwarded to U.S. attorneys in all fifty states and to the Justice Department's child exploitation and obscenity section in Washington, D.C.

THEY SAID IT . . .

"Technology is just a tool. In terms of getting the kids working together and motivating them, the teacher is the most important."
> BILL GATES

CHUCK'S CODE (FREEDOM)

Control that which seeks to control you. Take every thought captive. Master all things.

"When Chuck Norris plays Monopoly, it affects the world economy."

LET'S BE HONEST . . .

Of course, there's nothing funny about the tough economic times that so many around our country and world find themselves in today. My wife, Gena, and I sincerely pray all the time for those who are out of work or displaced by the loss of a home.

If I could encourage such people, I would admonish them not to lose hope, but to continue to look outside the box for a solution, to remember the roots of the American dream, and most of all, to ask God to help them. When I think about the adversity in which the Founding Fathers started this country, from Valley Forge to creating a government from scratch, I'm reminded of the hope that shines through wintry storms.

Our founders' voices stretch across time to remind us that,

even as we seek provision for our daily needs, we must simultaneously remember that happiness and true prosperity do not come from the things we have, the objects we accumulate, the size of our bank accounts, or big government handouts. As Benjamin Franklin once said, "Money never made a man happy yet, nor will it. . . . The more a man has, the more he wants. Instead of filling a vacuum, it makes one."

"In God We Trust" is inscribed on our money for a reason—so that we might never forget our true source of security. It comes first and foremost by trusting in God, our Creator, as the founders did.

There's a verse in the Bible that summarizes it for me: "Instruct those who are rich in this present world not to be conceited or to fix their hope on the uncertainty of riches, but on God, who richly supplies us with all things to enjoy."[1]

That is why Thomas Jefferson could say, "I sincerely pray that all the members of the human family may, in the time prescribed by the Father of us all, find themselves securely established in the enjoyment of life, liberty, and happiness."

And so do I.

THEY SAID IT . . .

"Sometimes by losing a battle you find a new way to win the war."

> DONALD TRUMP

CHUCK'S CODE (FREEDOM)

While we seek provision for our daily needs, we must simultaneously remember that happiness and true prosperity do not come from the things we have, the objects we accumulate, the size of our bank accounts, or big government handouts.

#27

OFFICIAL CHUCK NORRIS FACT

"Chuck Norris never won an Academy Award for acting in any of his action movies— because he's not acting."

LET'S BE HONEST . . .

I've never been one to worry about peer awards and accolades. For more than thirty years, I've received plenty of rewards for the movies I've made, yet my most valued prize comes simply from how the public has enjoyed them.

Lone Wolf McQuade is one of my favorite and most popular films. I didn't realize it at the time, but it was also a transition film for me. My previous movies had been based on my martial arts abilities, but *Lone Wolf* was a pure action-adventure picture. Admittedly, it felt a little strange at first, but then the motif grew on me and ultimately led and developed into the *Walker, Texas Ranger* series. Even my critics acknowledged that it was a big step forward for me. It was also a necessary step for me to make, if I were to grow in my profession as well as fulfill what God wanted for my life.

Transitions are tough because they have to do with change, and we all know that "the only person who likes change is a wet baby," as Mark Twain once said. But transitions are necessary because without them, we would hardly advance. Many times, we have no idea where the transition will lead us, but we do know there is no reward without the risk. You have to give up to go up.

Are you facing changes? a transition? Try not to fret too much. The road to the next level might be uphill. But I guarantee you that, when you arrive, life's vista there will be much better than where you are now.

THEY SAID IT . . .

"If we are to better the future, we must disturb the present."

> CATHERINE BOOTH, COFOUNDER OF THE SALVATION ARMY

CHUCK'S CODE (FIGHT)

You have to give up to go up.

"For undercover police work, Chuck Norris pins his badge underneath his shirt, directly onto his chest."

LET'S BE HONEST . . .

Speaking of police work, I read a great story recently that reminds us that crime never pays—and even if it does, you'll pay it back in the end.

On January 17, 1950, eleven men stole $2.7 million from the Brinks Armored Car depot in Boston, Massachusetts—quite a heist. It was the largest robbery at that time in the United States.

After eighteen months of preparation, Anthony "Fats" Pino and ten recruits, wearing navy blue coats, Halloween masks, and chauffeur's caps, entered the depot with counterfeit keys, tied up the employees, and filled fourteen canvas bags with lots and lots of loot. After a clean getaway, they split their spoil and made an oath not to touch the money until the statute of limitations ran out six years later.

It would have been a perfect crime, except for one minor glitch. When one of the men, Joseph "Specs" O'Keefe, went to prison to serve a separate sentence for burglary, he entrusted his share of the money to the others in the group. But while he was in jail, he threatened to tell the authorities if the others didn't send him money. A hit man was contracted to take out O'Keefe, but the would-be killer was caught. As a result, O'Keefe, who was wounded in the assault, made a deal with the FBI to rat out the other ten members of the group.

In January 1956, just days before the statute of limitations for the theft would have expired, six of the men were captured. In all, eight of them were tried and given life sentences. Two others died before they could go to trial.

As for the money, most of it was never found. The story is that it had been hidden in the hills north of Grand Rapids, Minnesota.[1]

Nearly every criminal feels that he is smarter than his victims. But this is just one reminder that, as Baretta used to say, "If you can't do the time, don't do the crime."

THEY SAID IT . . .
"Always do right. This will gratify some people and astonish the rest." > MARK TWAIN

CHUCK'S CODE (FREEDOM)
Crime never pays—and even if it does, you'll pay it back in the end.

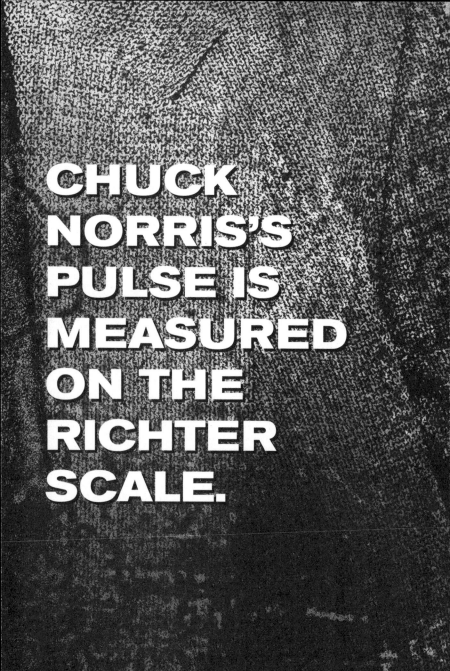

CHUCK NORRIS'S PULSE IS MEASURED ON THE RICHTER SCALE.

"Chuck Norris knows everything there is to know—except the definition of mercy."

LET'S BE HONEST . . .

After I finished filming *Code of Silence* in Chicago, I was invited to play in a celebrity soccer game in Florence, Italy, against an Italian celebrity team. The soccer field in Florence is the largest in the world.

When our American team arrived, we found out that the

Italian celebrities had been training for five months with the world-champion professional Italian team. Not knowing how to play the game, I was already nervous, but then I became very apprehensive.

The night of the game, there were over fifty thousand people in attendance. I thought, *They sure like their soccer*—or *futbol*, as they call it there. Our coach gave us some last-minute instructions, informing us to expect some cheap shots if we should happen to take the lead. I asked, "What kind of cheap shots?" He said, "They may check your leg, causing injury to your knee." I replied, "The first one who tries that on me will die right on the field!"

We went out on the field and met our opponents. After meeting the player who would be guarding me, I told him I had never played soccer before, and I knew that I couldn't use my hands, just my legs. So, I asked him, "Can I do this?" Then I snapped a side-kick, barely grazing his nose. His eyes widened, and he said, "No, no, you can't do that!" "Oh," I replied. "I was just wondering." During the game, that man wouldn't come near me, so I was able to pass the ball leisurely to my teammates.

The second half started with our team leading 1–0. I asked if I could sit out the second half and let the more experienced members of our team play. (The real reason was that, after chasing the ball all over the field for the first half, I felt like I had done the twenty-mile dash.) During the second half, one of our players came out of the game with a bloody nose. Then another player came off the field limping. Finally, our last reserve player came off holding his side.

The coach looked at me and shrugged. So I went back onto the field. Fortunately, I had the same guy guarding me. To the Italians' dismay, the game ended with us winning 1–0.

"If a team wants to intimidate you physically and you let them, they've won." > MIA HAMM, AMERICAN WORLD CUP SOCCER CHAMPION

CHUCK'S CODE (FIGHT)

T.E.A.M. = Together **E**veryone **A**chieves **M**ore

#30

OFFICIAL CHUCK NORRIS FACT

"Chuck Norris can kill two stones with one bird."

LET'S BE HONEST . . .

Multitasking is a term given to doing a few or many things at once. It's another way of expressing the old saying, "Kill two birds with one stone."

This concept lays the foundation for a commonly held belief that the more we can get done at once, the better off we are. But is that the truth?

In Dave Crenshaw's book *The Myth of Multitasking: How "Doing It All" Gets Nothing Done*, he demonstrates how multitasking is, in fact, a lie that actually wastes time, energy, and money. Most of all, it robs us of life and our relationships with others.

The facts show that switching tasks (or "switchtasking," as Dave calls it) not only uses up more of our resources, but it also diminishes our overall productivity, because it spreads us too thin and stretches us in more directions than we should go.

I heard a CEO once ask his corporate managers, "What are you called to do?" Many answered by elaborating on their job titles, positions, or descriptions. Others gave a litany of duties that any workaholic would be proud of.

When they finished giving their answers, which obviously missed the mark the CEO was looking for, he replied, "You're called to do the 5 percent that no one else can do because they are not you." He then went on to speak about each person's unique contributions.

We're not called to be everything to everyone. And we can't do everything. Despite the pull of our culture, we need to resist the tyranny of the urgent, limit our to-dos, and focus our energies and resources on doing the few things that we do well or only we can do, like "killing two stones with one bird."

THEY SAID IT . . .

"The main thing is to keep the main thing the main thing."
> STEPHEN R. COVEY

 **CHUCK'S CODE (FITNESS)**

We need to resist the tyranny of the urgent, limit our to-dos, and focus our energies and resources on doing the few things that we do well or only we can do.

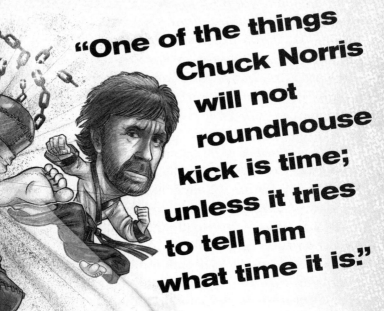

"One of the things Chuck Norris will not roundhouse kick is time; unless it tries to tell him what time it is."

LET'S BE HONEST . . .

My first big break was with the movie *Good Guys Wear Black*.
I helped to develop and write the screenplay, and I peddled it
around Hollywood for four years before I was able to finally make
it a reality.

Prior to that, I owned and operated three martial arts schools
that a company bought to take nationwide—a chain of Chuck Norris
schools. Two years later, I lost everything. It took me five years of giving seminars and teaching private lessons to avoid bankruptcy.

One of my private students was an actor by the name of Steve McQueen. He said, "I would suggest that you try the acting field."

I replied, "Why? I've never had an acting class in my life. I never even did a high school play."

Steve said, "Well, acting is not just having lessons. You either have a certain presence that comes across on the screen, or you don't. I think you may have it. I strongly suggest that you give it a try."

I thought about it for several months before I decided, because once I decide to do something, I'm not going to give up.

I checked into various acting schools, but they were all too expensive. Finally, I found a school that could be paid through my GI Bill.

So I began studying acting. But when I went out to find work as an actor, I was competing against guys with years and years of experience. I thought, *This isn't going to work*. So I decided to write my own screenplay. Through sheer determination and faith, the idea eventually sold and became a successful film. That was in 1977.

Sometimes life calls for a left turn on a red light. It never feels right. It rarely if ever is expected. And it often doesn't make sense. But when "the voice" calls to move, best get moving!

THEY SAID IT . . .
"Life is either a daring adventure or nothing at all."
> HELEN KELLER

CHUCK'S CODE (FIGHT)

Sometimes life calls for a left turn on a red light. It never feels right. It rarely if ever is expected. And it often doesn't make sense. But when "the voice" calls to move, best get moving!

"Remember the Soviet Union? They disbanded after watching a *Delta Force* marathon on satellite TV."

LET'S BE HONEST . . .

During a trip to the Russian Federation, my wife, Gena, and I were invited to visit a predominantly Mongolian republic called Kalmykia, located west of Kazakhstan. The president of the republic personally flew to Moscow to pick us up in his private jet.

As we deplaned in Elista, the capital city, we were greeted by a welcoming party of government officials and some of the local people. Three greeters welcomed each of us with a bowl of their local delicacy to drink—something that looked similar to milk.

I took a sip and nearly gagged. I later discovered that the drink was a mixture of warm horse's milk, butter, and salt. *Yuck!*

Our hosts were eager to show us their culture and how the Mongolians had lived in earlier times. We viewed the tents once used for housing, their pig-roasting pits, and Mongolian warriors' superior skills with the bow. They also took us out to an archery range, where they put on a demonstration, shooting arrows into a circular bull's-eye with great accuracy and skill.

One of the men brought a bow and arrow over for me to try out my skills. So I pulled back on the bowstring and immediately realized it was no toy. It took considerable strength to draw it back.

I was about fifty feet away from the target as I pulled back the bow and let the arrow fly. What happened next was a total God moment. It struck the bull's-eye dead center! My mouth dropped wide-open. Gena screamed, "You hit the bull's-eye!" I whispered back to her, "I hope they don't ask me to do that again."

THEY SAID IT . . .

"To me, the definition of focus is knowing exactly where you want to be today, next week, next month, next year, and then never deviating from your plan. Once you can see, touch, and feel your objective, all you have to do is pull back and put all your strength behind it, and you'll hit your target every time." > BRUCE JENNER, OLYMPIC CHAMPION

CHUCK'S CODE (FIGHT)

It is important to have a goal in mind. Accept the fact that there will be setbacks and obstacles. But if you continue to visualize that goal and work toward it, one day you will achieve it.

#33

OFFICIAL CHUCK
NORRIS FACT

"America is not a democracy. It's a Chucktatorship."

LET'S BE HONEST . . .

People are always asking me to run for some form of government office. In fact, right now there are some fans on the Internet proposing I run for president in 2012. They're trying to accumulate one million signatures to get the ball rolling.

Of course, I really appreciate their confidence in me, but I have no desire to run for any office. I can get more accomplished for the greater good now than I ever could as an elected official.

I am concerned about the future of our country, and I wrote about it in my book *Black Belt Patriotism*. I also address my concerns weekly in my syndicated column, available in various publications across the country and online on such news and opinion blogs as *WorldNetDaily*, *Town Hall*, and *Human Events*.

When someone approaches me about running, say, for governor, I will ask them this question: "Let's say I'm debating my opponent on national television, and he starts attacking my character. So I fly over the table and choke him unconscious. Do you think that will help my campaign?"

Generally they say, "I don't think so." But some have replied, "It might!"

You see, I'm not going to take any bull from arrogant politicians. My skin is just not that thick.

Sometimes I wish this Fact were true, because then I could go to Washington, D.C., line up all the members of Congress side by side and ask Ron Paul (who I believe is one of the most honest members of Congress) to point out the dishonest members. I would then walk up to each individual that Ron Paul pointed out as dishonest, stare him in the eye, and say, "You're fired." If he didn't move immediately, I would choke him unconscious and drag him over to the side.

Of course, if Ron pointed out a female member of Congress as being dishonest, I would walk up to her, look her in the eye, and say, "You're fired," but I would personally escort her out, because I'm a Texas gentleman.

I have told this humorous story repeatedly on television and radio. But, honestly, I do wish Congress would take the concerns of the American people to heart more than their own selfish concerns and special interests.

THEY SAID IT . . .

"*Politics* is made up of two words: *poli*, which is Greek for 'many,' and *tics*, which are bloodsucking insects." > GORE VIDAL

CHUCK'S CODE (FREEDOM)

One of your most important civic duties is to keep your representatives accountable to and aligned with the Constitution. And if they will not, vote them out.

OFFICIAL CHUCK NORRIS FACT #34

"To eliminate obsolete pennies, Chuck Norris stretches them into $5 bills— since Lincoln is on both anyway."

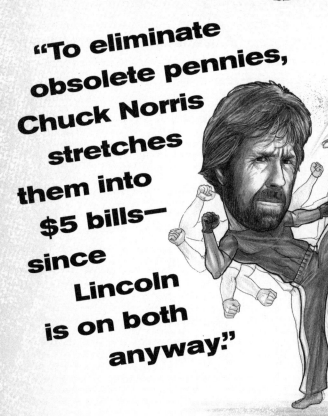

LET'S BE HONEST . . .

I really wish I could turn every penny into five dollars for every person that truly needs more money or is experiencing economic hardship.

I'm not a financial counselor, but I am a businessman who has learned the value of fiscal prudence and who depends on the wise counsel of others. I've come to really appreciate the sound advice of Dave Ramsey, not only for his printed resources, but also for the wealth of information on his Web site (www.daveramsey.com). Dave even has some great resources for young people.[1] I also recommend my friend Randy Alcorn's *Money, Possessions, and Eternity* for an eternal perspective on money matters.[2]

There are some fundamentals we all should practice. Whether we're young or old, these basics should always be reflected in our bank books.

First, be willing to work. Strive to achieve your desired position, but don't be too proud to take what's available. Even in times of employment drought, there is always someone who needs something done. It might not be your ideal job, but work is work.

Second, live within your means. We are inundated in a culture that saturates us with extravagant living. But if we're ever to get where we need to be, we'll need financial restraint and discipline to get there. Be content with what you have. And don't spend what you don't have.

Third, save. Proverbs 6:6-8 advises us to "take a lesson from the ants," who "labor hard all summer gathering food for the winter."[3] Many people often say they don't have enough money to save, but the truth is they've often overextended themselves. Even if it's only a small amount, try to set aside some money each month for safekeeping.

Fourth, give. Selfishness is a struggle for all of us. Giving helps us remember that we're not alone, and it often puts our difficulties into a proper perspective. Moreover, a spirit of poverty is often broken by a spirit of generosity. We might not have an overflow of treasures, but we always have some time and talents to offer.

Just as it's true in relationships and other areas of life, so it's true with our finances: Go back to the basics. You're a steward of all that God has given you—time, talents, and other resources. When all else fails, recall that ol' K.I.S.S. method: Keep It Simple—Simon says! (You were expecting something different?)

THEY SAID IT . . .
"If broke people are making fun of your financial plan, you're on track." > DAVE RAMSEY

 CHUCK'S CODE (FREEDOM)

Live within your means; learn to save and invest.

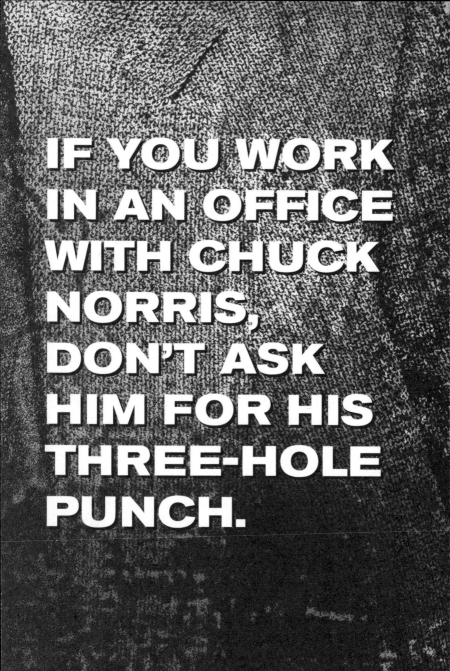

"There is no such thing as evolution. Just a list of creatures Chuck Norris has allowed to live."

LET'S BE HONEST . . .

I'm no science buff, but I love reading about the sciences and new scientific discoveries. I view the field much like men of old did: Science is the observational study of God's creation.

Naturalistic views of science have prompted some people

to call into question the existence of a Creator or Intelligent Designer. Darwinism and its offshoots have almost single-handedly dethroned humans as the highest pedestal of creation and made it seem as if we are nothing more than a product of random chance—no different from a kangaroo or cockroach.

Don't misunderstand me. I believe in microevolution, genetic mutations that provide small variations in different species in the animal kingdom. But I don't believe those micro-mutations lead to macroevolution, large genetic jumps that turn one animal into another, such as apes into humans.

Regardless of one's beliefs about evolution, the theory in any form does not disprove the existence of a Creator. In fact, hundreds of scientists have acknowledged belief in an Intelligent Designer.[1]

And why don't others? Phillip E. Johnson, the Berkeley professor who wrote *Darwin on Trial*, answered that question when he said, "The problem with allowing God a role in the history of life is not that science would cease, but rather that scientists would have to acknowledge the existence of something important which is outside the boundaries of natural science."[2]

The truth is that the life you see on earth is really just a list of creatures *God* has allowed to live. We are not creations of random chance. We are not accidents. There is a God, a Creator, who made you and me. You are special. You are unique. We were all made in God's image, created to be stewards of this planet, which is what separates us from all other creatures.

THEY SAID IT . . .

"Statements about ancestry and descent are not applicable in the fossil record. . . . It is easy enough to make up stories of how one form gave rise to another, and to find reasons why the stages should be favored by natural selection. But such stories are not part of science, for there is no way of putting them to the test."

> DR. COLIN PATTERSON, SENIOR PALEONTOLOGIST AT THE BRITISH MUSEUM OF NATURAL HISTORY[3]

 CHUCK'S CODE (FAITH)

As you value yourself, so you will live and treat others.

"Chuck Norris can eat just one Lay's potato chip."

LET'S BE HONEST . . .

Like many people, I try to maintain good eating habits. But, for example, if I'm watching a football game with a big bag of potato chips, I can tear the bag open during the first quarter and ask myself by halftime (while licking the salt from my fingertips), "What's this empty bag doing in my lap?" I won't even tell you how quickly a bowl of ice cream can disappear during the second half!

I'm a believer in new beginnings. That's why I'm an advocate of New Year's resolutions. The potential to fail is always present. But so is the potential to succeed and soar to the next level. Studies show that our successes actually happen more often than we think.

A University of Washington survey conducted several years ago showed that 63 percent of the people questioned were still keeping their number one resolution after two months. That's great and hope-filled news.

"The keys to making a successful resolution are a person's confidence that he or she can make the behavior[al] change and the commitment to making that change," said the study. "Resolutions are a process, not a one-time effort that offer people a chance to create new habits."[1]

So whether you want to exercise more, lose weight, stop smoking, cut down on alcohol, make a new spiritual commitment, or make new friends, don't ever quit striving to better yourself each and every year.

If you stick to your commitments, I believe you, too, will find the power and discipline to eat just one Lay's potato chip!

THEY SAID IT . . .
"Be always at war with your vices, at peace with your neighbors, and let each new year find you a better man."
> BENJAMIN FRANKLIN

⬤ CHUCK'S CODE (FITNESS)

The potential to fail is always present. But so is the potential to succeed and soar to the next level.

"Chuck Norris grinds his coffee with his teeth and boils the water with his rage."

LET'S BE HONEST . . .

One evening in the late 1980s, I attended a Los Angeles Kings hockey game with some friends, Mary Hart, host of *Entertainment Tonight*, and her husband, Burt Sugarman, a very successful entrepreneur and an owner of Rally's, a fast-food chain.

After the game was over, Burt asked, "Why don't we stop at Rally's in Inglewood and pick up some hamburgers?" Mary and I agreed.

When we arrived at Rally's, Burt pulled into the parking lot, right in between two rival gangs that were standing around their vans and staring at each other while a boom box blasted music.

Burt stopped, uncertain about what to do. He knew there had been a gang killing in that very parking lot just a month earlier.

I told him to pull into a parking space, which he did. We then got out of the car and walked right between the gangs and their vans, as if nothing were going on.

We walked up to the take-out window and ordered our food. As we did, the gang with the boom box turned down the music, and I could hear my name being mentioned.

As we waited for our order, one of the gang members walked over to me and asked if I was Chuck Norris. I told him I was. He then yelled out to the other guys, "Yeah, he is Chuck Norris!" When he said that, several other members of his gang came over.

As we were shooting the breeze, the opposing gang came over, too, and everyone mingled together, listening to me talk about my film and martial arts careers.

After Burt, Mary, and I received our hamburgers, I shook hands with all the gang members. As we walked back to the car, the two gangs got into their vans and drove off.

Burt was so impressed by what transpired that night that, whenever he gave a speech after that, he would tell the audience how Chuck Norris stopped a gang war in a Rally's parking lot!

"Unity to be real must stand the severest strain without breaking."

> MAHATMA GANDHI

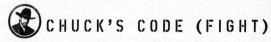

CHUCK'S CODE (FIGHT)

Face your fears and conquer them. Fight your prejudices, not others. To quote the motto for my new America Remembers collector's edition Colt .45 revolver: "Men are like steel. When they lose their temper, they lose their worth."[1]

"Dynamite was originally developed by Chuck Norris to cure his indigestion."

LET'S BE HONEST . . .

One of my favorite films is *Pirates of the Caribbean*. Actors who play pirates in movies are interesting characters. Real pirates, however, hardly fit the glamour that Hollywood gives them. We've recently learned that again by observing the actions of Somali pirates, many of whom are merely marauding mobs of teens.

In March 2009, Somali pirates hijacked a cargo ship with twenty American crew members on board. During 2008 alone, more than 130 vessels were attacked off the coast of Somalia, resulting in fifty successful hijackings and millions of dollars paid in ransoms.

Some might not know that the United States has been dealing with African marauding mariners since our inception. While the young nation was mopping up from the Revolutionary War, we were also squaring off against Barbary pirates in the Mediterranean Sea. These sea bandits cruised the coastlines, stealing cargo, destroying villages, and enslaving millions of Africans and hundreds of thousands of Europeans and Americans.

America's first four presidents (Washington, Adams, Jefferson, and Madison) dealt with this conflict of powers in various ways. From roughly 1784 to 1801, the American government gave millions of dollars in ransoms to these radicals, including an estimated 20 percent of our federal budget in 1800! (Men such as Thomas Jefferson argued vehemently against paying ransoms and tribute. Jefferson believed that the only road to resolution would be through the "medium of war.")

America's founders believed in a foreign policy of nonintervention, but Jefferson realized that protecting America's borders also meant protecting American lives and property overseas. He confessed to Congress in 1801 that he was "unauthorized by the Constitution, without the sanction of Congress, to go beyond the line of defense,"[1] but he still ordered a small fleet of warships to the Mediterranean to ward off attacks by the Barbary States.

> *"From the Halls of Montezuma,*
> *To the shores of Tripoli;*
> *We fight our country's battles*
> *In the air, on land, and sea."*

> "THE MARINES' HYMN," COMMEMORATING AMERICA'S VICTORY
OVER MEDITERRANEAN PIRATES IN THE FOUNDING DECADES OF OUR
REPUBLIC

CHUCK'S CODE (FREEDOM)

Never underestimate an opponent. You can be defeated as
easily by overconfidence on your part as by his skill.

"SWEATING BULLETS" IS LITERALLY WHAT HAPPENS WHEN CHUCK NORRIS GETS TOO HOT.

"Chuck Norris
stared evil
in the eye,
and it went into
hiding."

LET'S BE HONEST . . .

Evil pervades society, and there's no clearer place to see its menac-
ing claws than in how it tears apart families. If statistics are any indi-
cation, you've likely felt the jaws of evil clamp down on your own
family. It rips apart relationships and breaks hearts at the same time.

The traditional family is under assault. Today, the traditional
family has become one option among many, as cohabitation con-
quers the cultural landscape. More than twelve million people now

cohabitate in the United States, and only half of those are likely to ever marry each other. Forty percent of babies today are born to unmarried women, compared to only 3.8 percent in 1940. Times were not always this complicated.

I might sound a bit old-fashioned, but I still believe that a family consists of a mom, a dad, and some kids. I also still believe that families can survive and thrive through the darkest of times.

You might have been deeply affected by divorce or even endured abandonment by a parent (or something worse), but I'm here to encourage you that God can turn around what others meant for harm and use it for good. I'm proof of that, having survived an alcoholic, abusive, and philandering father, and having helped my mother raise my two younger brothers. The things I had to endure as a child strengthened me to persevere later in life as I worked to succeed in my martial arts, movie, and television careers.

Every family tree has its nuts, but it likely has at least some fruit to enjoy as well. And even if it doesn't, you can always enjoy the fruit of being a part of God's family. The Psalms are a constant reminder that "God is a father to the fatherless . . . and makes a home for the lonely."[1]

THEY SAID IT . . .

"A family is a unit composed not only of children but of men, women, an occasional animal, and the common cold."

> OGDEN NASH

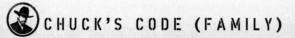

CHUCK'S CODE (FAMILY)

Fighting for your family is a fight worth fighting.

"Chuck Norris traveled back in time and wrote the Declaration of Independence, but he gave the credit to Thomas Jefferson."

LET'S BE HONEST . . .

Do you know what happened to the fifty-six men who signed the Declaration of Independence? For a number of years, an e-mail was widely circulated with partial truths, some history, some legend, and some falsehoods about these men of valor. But here's the real scoop.

Thomas McKean wrote to John Adams in 1777 that he was "hunted like a fox by the enemy, compelled to [move] my family five times in three months."

Five signers were captured by the British as prisoners of war and had to endure the deplorable conditions as such. One signer lost his son in the Revolutionary Army, and another had two sons captured.

At least twelve signers had their homes and property taken, ransacked, occupied, or burned. Vandals or soldiers looted the properties of William Ellery, George Clymer, Lyman Hall, George Walton, Button Gwinnett, Thomas Heyward Jr., Edward Rutledge, and Arthur Middleton. Francis Lewis had his home and property destroyed. The enemy jailed his wife, and she was held for months before being exchanged for wives of British soldiers. John Hart's farm was looted, and he had to flee into hiding. Robert Morris's home was overtaken as well, and Philip Livingston lost several properties to the enemy. Carter Braxton of Virginia, a wealthy planter and trader, lost his ships and cargo to the British navy.[1]

And that's just a sampling of what these men sacrificed.

Like a host of other Americans in that age, the signers of the Declaration of Independence paid a price for freedom. Though the war actually started a year before their signing, what they did testified to the risks they were willing to take. And though all their misfortunes cannot be directly linked to their signing of the Declaration, they represent the untold costs paid by the patriots during the Revolutionary War. They collectively stood together and pledged with conviction: "For the support of this Declaration, with a firm reliance on the protection of divine Providence, we mutually pledge to each other our Lives, our Fortunes and our sacred Honor."[2]

One thing is for sure: All the signers sacrificed something to give us an independent America. What price are we willing to pay to keep it?

THEY SAID IT . . .

"We must all hang together, or most assuredly we shall all hang separately." > BENJAMIN FRANKLIN

CHUCK'S CODE (FREEDOM)

All the signers of the Declaration of Independence sacrificed something to give us an independent America. What price are we willing to pay to keep it?

"Chuck Norris was here. 11/2/06"

(written by Chuck on the wall of a Navy SEALs barrack in Fallujah, Iraq, during his first visit)

"Chuck Norris was here again! 9/15/07"

(written by Chuck on the same wall ten months later, during his second visit)

LET'S BE HONEST . . .

In 2007, as I was touring American bases and camps in Iraq, shaking hands and taking pictures with our troops, I had the opportunity to sit down and talk to a group of Navy SEALs in Fallujah.

Two of the men were reenlisting, and they asked their commander if I could read them their oath. The commander agreed, and they repeated what I read to them. As I got to the end of the oath, I said to them, "So help me God," and they responded, "So help me Chuck Norris."

My chaplain toured Iraq with me, and he was there watching. I looked at him, my face beet red. I wondered what I should do and whether God was going to hold this against me. The two SEALs finally got me off the hook by saying, "So help me God." They were all laughing at my shocked expression.

I also recall seeing a large billboard message at Al Asad Air Base in Iraq that read: "Chuck Norris is here." The following day, after my visit, the words were added: "Chuck Norris has always been here; he just now decided to reveal himself."

I am truly honored, humbled, and proud to have played a small part in our troops' inspiration, even humor. If something encourages them and puts a smile on their faces, count me in.

Whether you're abroad or Stateside, I encourage you to put into practice something I did in Iraq and try to do every time I see servicemen or women in uniform anywhere. I stop them, look them in the eyes, shake their hands, and say, "Thank you for your service."

"Also remember that in any man's dark hour, a pat on the back and an earnest handclasp may work a small miracle."

> BRIGADIER GENERAL S. L. A. MARSHALL, *THE ARMED FORCES OFFICER* (1950)

CHUCK'S CODE (FREEDOM)

Stop servicemen and women, look them in the eyes, shake their hands, and say, "Thank you for your service."

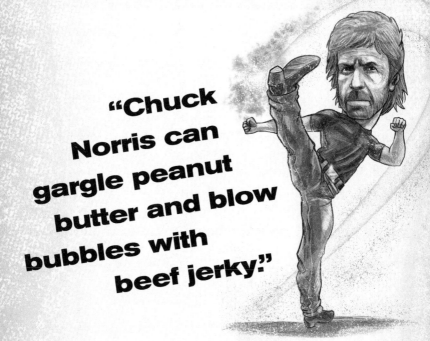

"Chuck Norris can gargle peanut butter and blow bubbles with beef jerky."

LET'S BE HONEST . . .

Just reading this Fact made me want a glass of milk! Actually, I love peanut butter, especially on toast with banana slices.

To be honest with you, my wife, Gena, is the one who keeps our family on a healthy regimen. She is an avid reader of anything related to health and nutrition.

Here's a little inside view of what our daily diet looks like: We eat lots of whole foods, mostly organic. We keep fresh fruit and vegetables readily available to snack on. I realize it is more costly to buy foods of this kind, but when you consider the cost of long-term disease and health care, it is a much smaller investment in the long run—and you will feel better for it. And don't forget the water. I try to carry a bottle with me at all times.

For breakfast, we try to eat a balanced diet of protein and whole grains. It is important to start the day off with something very healthy and not to skip that meal. A good breakfast jump-starts your metabolism, feeds your brain, balances your blood sugar, and supplies you with sustained energy. It is typical for our family to eat a peanut butter and banana sandwich on sprouted grain bread for breakfast. This provides lots of energy, and our twins love it too.

Lunch is usually tuna fish (in moderation, because of mercury levels) or avocado sandwiches. We try to eat dinner by five or five thirty, and no later than six. We try not to eat many complex carbo-hydrates at night either: at most a small red baked potato or about a half cup of brown rice. We try to eat a lot of rich, green steamed vegetables or fresh romaine salads with lots of color, along with a six-ounce piece of baked, skinless, free-range chicken breast or salmon.

In our diet, we try to live by the words of Hippocrates, who said, "Our food should be our medicine, and our medicine should be our food."

Of course, everyone has to splurge once in a while. Like my kids, I enjoy a good bowl of Blue Bell ice cream. And I have to confess that, when Gena and I see a movie, I can't watch it without a bag of popcorn (non-buttered, of course).

THEY SAID IT . . .

"Vegetarians are cool. All I eat are vegetarians—except for the occasional mountain lion steak." > TED NUGENT

 CHUCK'S CODE (FITNESS)

You are what you eat, so conquer the consumptive war!

"When Chuck Norris was an infant, his parents gave him a toy hammer. He gave the world Stonehenge."

LET'S BE HONEST . . .

I've felt honored to be reconnected to the younger generations through the Chuck Norris Fact phenomenon. I hear from thousands of you every year, listen to your concerns, and do my best to carry those concerns to the appropriate parties to implement change.

It doesn't take a political scientist to realize that you, the next generation of young people to bear the baton of America, are carrying unique and heavy burdens.

You have grown up with technology. You use it for everything from listening to music, to getting jobs, to ordering everything you need, to dating and communicating with everyone you know and want to know. You are tired of wars, rumors of wars, and America's mentality that it must save the world. You prefer to feed the poor and encourage the downtrodden. You believe that charity begins at home. (The Lord knows we have millions of people in America who need our assistance.) Your primary fight is socially conscious service. In your eyes, government is some gargantuan gargoyle that is spiraling out of control.

Your generation has so much to offer our world. If we're going to win our culture wars, we need you to do it. There is no way around it.

You might be overwhelmed by the amount of change that needs to take place. But, as the adage goes, wars are won one battle at a time. And there's nothing more worthy to fight for than for God and country.

Don't ever feel as if your contributions are too small. Every little bit counts. No effort will prove unproductive. As it says in the Bible, "Stand firm. Let nothing move you. Always give yourselves fully to the work of the Lord, because you know that your labor in the Lord is not in vain."[1]

THEY SAID IT . . .

"So we have to first ask the question—how can we take all this wealth and give it away? All the technology and beautiful parts of capitalism and bless the world and the poor—or else we're in deep trouble." > ROB BELL[2]

CHUCK'S CODE (FREEDOM)

I will always be in a positive frame of mind and convey this feeling to every person I meet. (#3 of my Principles for Life)

WHEN CHUCK NORRIS WAS BORN, THE DOCTOR WAS THE ONLY ONE WHO CRIED

NEVER SLAP CHUCK NORRIS

OFFICIAL CHUCK
NORRIS FACT

"When you say, 'No one is perfect,' Chuck Norris takes it as a personal insult."

LET'S BE HONEST . . .

I know this might come as a shock to some, but no one is perfect—especially me. But life isn't about being perfect; it's about discovering who you are and not allowing others to devalue your real worth.

Most people would never allow someone to tell them that their new car was worth only pennies on the dollar, but that is exactly how we sell ourselves out every time we believe, accept, or perpetuate the lies that we are only as good as we look, what we do, or what we own.

From name-brand clothing to positions of importance, the world tries to press us all into a mold that, in the end, understates or under-appraises our true value—the true worth of every human being.

I believe we've devalued human life—so much so that it affects the way we treat one another. We've discarded our ancestral beliefs that give value to people as distinct from, and higher than, the animals by virtue of our being made in the very image of God.

Even the early Americans who adhered to Deism believed in a Creator and that humans were the highest creation of God. That is why the founders wrote in the Declaration of Independence, "We hold these truths to be self-evident, that all men are created equal, that they are endowed by their Creator with certain unalienable rights, that among these are life, liberty, and the pursuit of happiness." Though culture would have to catch up with this national creed, inherent within those words was equality for slaves, women, and even the unborn.

For better or worse, times have changed in many ways since our founders' day, and so has the way we view the essence of humanity. We have not only abandoned an early American worldview of humanity, but a biblical one as well.

Without a divine blueprint for life, the value of humanity is now tragically appraised solely on the basis of material worth, societal positions, cultural contributions, perceived quality of life, etc. And the result is that, today, human life is too easily regarded as disposable—fostered by our continual debate about when life begins and ends.

The truth is, you were created in the image of God—you reflect the very nature of the Creator.[1] You are a child of God. And if we looked through those valued lenses at ourselves and others, we might treat one another again as the kings and queens we were created to be.

I believe it is not only the call of government but also the challenge of all Americans to believe as Thomas Jefferson did: "The care of human life and happiness, and not their destruction, is the first and only legitimate object of good government."[2] If we appraise one another's true human worth, and pass that value on in action, we will not only better ourselves but also our country.

THEY SAID IT . . .

"You come of the Lord Adam and the Lady Eve. . . . And that is both honour enough to erect the head of the poorest beggar, and shame enough to bow the shoulders of the greatest emperor on earth." > ASLAN, IN C. S. LEWIS'S *PRINCE CASPIAN*

 CHUCK'S CODE (FAITH)

I will look for the good in all people and make them feel worthwhile. (#5 of my Principles for Life)

"Chuck Norris eats bullets for breakfast. Watch out when he burps!"

LET'S BE HONEST . . .

When I was filming *Missing in Action 2: The Beginning* in St. Kitts in the Caribbean, I played a prisoner of war in a small camp in Vietnam with six other prisoners. For one scene, a guard dragged me out of my cell, and the Viet Cong were going to hang me up by my feet, tie my hands behind my back, and then put a large mountain rat in a sack, tie it around my neck, and let the rat have a field day with my face.

The way the scene should have worked was for the prop

master to obtain a realistic stuffed rat that looked just like the real ones that had been captured and caged. Unfortunately, the fake rat did not show up on location.

Realizing how important the scene was, I had one of the live rats killed to be used as the needed prop. But I had to figure out how I could hold this rat in my mouth without catching some horrible disease.

I tried tape, but it wouldn't stick. I tried several other tricks, but to no avail. Finally, frustrated and with my temper getting the best of me, I yelled, "Forget it! Pull me up by my feet, and when I put the rat in my mouth, put the sack over my head and tie it on."

When they did that, I started thrashing around like the rat was attacking my face. We had fake blood running down the rope that went into the sack, and you could see the blood seeping out of the sack.

This went on for a couple of minutes, and then I stopped moving. They took the sack off my head, and I had the dead rat in my mouth. The rat and I were both covered in blood.

The scene went well. Thank goodness, because I did not want to do a second take!

THEY SAID IT . . .

"No animals were harmed in the recording of this episode. We tried, but that . . . monkey was just too fast." > STEPHEN COLBERT

CHUCK'S CODE (FITNESS)

Regarding the rat, do as I say, not as I do.

#46

"Chuck Norris can build a snowman out of rain."

LET'S BE HONEST . . .

I don't know about building a snowman out of rain, but we all know about someone who built a country through snow and rain. I'm referring to Washington in the winter at Valley Forge, of course.

No one typifies courage better than George Washington and the Continental Army, especially as they squared off against the redcoats at Valley Forge. They model for us how we must be as we face our own winter valleys in the culture wars. As the historians at the National Park Service recount, "Valley Forge was not the darkest hour of the Revolutionary War; it is a place where an already accomplished group of professionals stood their ground, honed their craft, and thwarted one of the major British offensives of the war."[1]

The courage and tenacity shown at Valley Forge serve as an inspiring example to all of us who stay the course in hope of gaining victory on the battlefields of the culture wars. With secular progressivism looming like the British army, it is only by forging through difficult days ahead that we will win the war. There are no promises at the moment. No visions of grandeur. Just some battle-scarred and wearied soldiers living in what our enemies know are humble, conservative huts.

These are long nights of the soul. And like at Valley Forge, some are singing patriotic songs. Others are gathering logs to provide more permanent dwelling places. A few remain downtrodden and convinced there is no hope of winning the present battle, let alone the war. And yet some see revival on the horizon, brought about by a new regiment of culture warriors being called to the battle line, to bear the patriots' burdens and fulfill their mission on the field of valor.

I once heard it said that it took only 2 percent of our

population to create our nation and that it still would take only 2 percent to change it today. If you don't like what you see in America today, join me by being a part of the new 2 percent!

THEY SAID IT . . .

"Is it the Fourth?" > LAST WORDS OF THOMAS JEFFERSON, THE THIRD U.S. PRESIDENT, WHO DIED JULY 4, 1826, THE VERY SAME DAY THAT JOHN ADAMS, THE SECOND U.S. PRESIDENT, DIED, AND FIFTY YEARS TO THE DAY AFTER THEY AND FIFTY-FOUR OTHERS ADOPTED THE DECLARATION OF INDEPENDENCE

 CHUCK'S CODE (FREEDOM)

We are the new regiment of culture warriors being called to the battle line to bear the patriots' burdens and fulfill their mission on the field of valor.

"When Chuck Norris exercises, the machine gets stronger."

LET'S BE HONEST . . .

Most people know that I endorse the Total Gym.[1] What they might not know is how I was introduced to that great exercise machine.

I actually learned about the Total Gym by chance. I had pulled a rotator cuff lifting weights, and I was going to have it operated on.

☆ **129** ☆

About that time I got a call from Larry Westfall and Tom Campanaro, who had just developed their machine for rehab centers.

They told me that the Total Gym could rehab my shoulder and that I wouldn't need the operation. I was skeptical, but I decided to give it a try. Tom and Larry came to my home, set up the machine, and showed me the exercises they wanted me to do. They said to try it for six weeks and see how I felt. So I did.

In six weeks, my shoulder was healed, and I was able to resume my jujitsu training. I remember thinking to myself, *I feel stronger and more flexible.* I finally realized it was my exercising on the Total Gym that did it.

I called Tom and Larry and told them that the Total Gym not only rehabbed my rotator cuff but also increased my strength. They said, "Sure, because of the elongated movements on the Total Gym, it not only builds up muscle strength, but tendon strength as well." That was 1976. I've now been working out with the Total Gym for thirty-three years, and it's as much a part of my life as my martial arts training has been since 1960.

THEY SAID IT . . .

"That's me. Six years and six hundred pounds ago . . . before I knew how much I hated myself. But that all changed once I founded Globo Gym." > WHITE GOODMAN (BEN STILLER'S CHARACTER IN THE MOVIE *DODGEBALL*)

CHUCK'S CODE (FITNESS)

Movement is medicine for the body. So move it!

"Chuck Norris can dribble a football."

LET'S BE HONEST . . .

In 1967, being the number one martial arts fighter in America, I was asked to fight in a tournament in Silver Springs, Maryland. I accepted the invitation. In these tournaments, the competitors would line up and fight whoever was in line next to them.

The young man next to me had just earned his black belt, and I was to be his first fight. He knew I was the top fighter in the country, and he was so nervous that he had to dash to the bathroom—he was sick to his stomach. When he came out of the bathroom, I walked over, put my arm around him, and said, "Don't worry. You'll do just fine."

When we got into the ring, I was still feeling sorry for him and mentally planned to ease up on him. The result: He beat me! And it was my own fault. I had underestimated my opponent.

True champions can deal with their failures as well as their successes, and they learn from both.

A good example of this is Tim Tebow, the Heisman Trophy–winning quarterback of the University of Florida Gators.

During the 2008 season, the Gators beat their first few opponents quite handily and appeared to be on a roll—until they played unranked Ole Miss and lost 31–30. After the game, Tim Tebow went before the cameras and the press and took the blame for the loss. He promised that from that day forward he would give 1,000 percent of his effort on every play and not let his team down again. That's exactly what he did, and they did not lose another game. The Gators went on to win the BCS Championship.

For his commitment to excellence, Tim Tebow is a true champion.

THEY SAID IT . . .

"A hero is an ordinary individual who finds the strength to persevere and endure in spite of overwhelming obstacles."

> CHRISTOPHER REEVE

CHUCK'S CODE (FITNESS)

I will forget the mistakes of the past and press on to greater achievements. (#2 of my Principles for Life)

OFFICIAL CHUCK
NORRIS FACT **#49**

"Chuck Norris sleeps with a pillow under his gun."

LET'S BE HONEST . . .

This past year I shot (no pun intended) an NRA public service announcement in which I shared my conviction about self-defense: "If some thug breaks into my home, I could use my roundhouse kick. But I prefer he look down the barrel of my gun."[1]

The reason I was so adamant in that PSA is because there has been some movement in our country to get away from our Second Amendment rights.

Last year, the Supreme Court even wrangled over the question, Should the government allow private citizens or only public servants ("state militias") "to keep and bear arms"?[2]

☆ **133** ☆

Is someone joking? Could the twenty-seven words of the Second Amendment be any clearer? "A well regulated militia being necessary to the security of a free state, the right *of the people* to keep and bear arms, shall not be infringed" (emphasis added).

Just because Washington, D.C., had a pistol problem (with their ban on handguns), the court shouldn't penalize the rest of the country by resetting national precedent based upon a biased Constitutional interpretation. The Bill of Rights either encompasses the privileges of every citizen in every amendment or none at all. In the early days of our country, many states had gun laws that aligned with the Constitutional standard.[3]

As Chief Justice John Roberts asked, "If it is limited to state militias, why would they say 'the right of the people'? . . . What is reasonable about a total ban on possession?"[4]

Thomas Jefferson similarly wrote near the end of his life in 1823, "On every question of construction [of the Constitution], carry ourselves back to the time when the Constitution was adopted, recollect the spirit manifested in the debates, and instead of trying what meaning may be squeezed out of the text, or invented against it, conform to the probable one in which it was passed."[5]

THEY SAID IT . . .

"Let your gun therefore be the constant companion of your walks."

> THOMAS JEFFERSON, IN A LETTER TO HIS NEPHEW PETER CARR[6]

CHUCK'S CODE (FREEDOM)

The right of the people to keep and bear arms shall not be infringed.

"The quickest way to a man's heart is with Chuck Norris's fist."

LET'S BE HONEST . . .

As a martial arts instructor for fifteen years before getting into the film industry, I saw how teaching children helped them overcome many of their insecurities. But these were kids whose parents could afford the cost of a commercial martial arts school. What about the millions of children whose parents could not afford it? I wondered how I could help them. That "how?" became a reality when President George H. W. Bush helped me launch a program in Houston, Texas, called "**KICKSTART KIDS**." Since 1992, we have graduated more than sixty thousand young people in the program. It has become Gena's and my life mission.

　　KICKSTART KIDS (www.kickstartkids.org) is a character-building life-skills program whose fundamental purpose is to give our nation's students the tools to strengthen their self-image. When a child develops a strong sense of self-awareness and inner strength, he or she is able to resist peer pressure, including drug and alcohol use and involvement in gangs. In addition, martial arts training provides young people with the core values and philosophies associated with leading a productive and healthy life. That is what we are all about: giving every child a chance for a productive life in which he or she can make healthy decisions and achieve his or her goals and dreams. It is our vision to someday have this prevention program in every middle school in America. I want to see the six thousand students we currently have multiply into millions of students throughout the country. If we can get the funding, we hope to do just that.

I am often given recognition for the ways **KICKSTART KIDS** helps young people, but the real heroes of the program are the **KICKSTART KIDS** instructors, who so unselfishly invest their time and energy into the lives of our youth every day. I consider them my heroes as well.

THEY SAID IT . . .

"I am only one, but I am one. I cannot do everything, but I can do something. And that which I can do, by the grace of God, I will do." > EDWARD EVERETT HALE

CHUCK'S CODE (FREEDOM)

A man's life is built not upon the years he has lived, but on the legacy he leaves.

"Chuck Norris will never have a heart attack; his heart isn't foolish enough to attack him."

LET'S BE HONEST . . .

Bob Barker, the well-known former host of *The Price Is Right*, called me after the movie *Happy Gilmore* was released in theaters. He asked if I had seen the movie and his fight scene with Adam Sandler.

"I sure did."

"So what did you think of the fight?" he asked.

"I could not have done better myself," I said.

Bob was a great martial arts student of mine, and he showed some of his superb technique in *Happy Gilmore.*

A while ago, I was reading a CNN report that spoke about Bob's heart condition at the time. The article poked fun at me, saying, "The price of taking karate lessons from martial arts maven Chuck Norris may have been a little too high."[1]

In his own words, Barker commented on his heart condition by saying, "Maybe I should blame it on Chuck Norris. He probably kicked me in the neck. God knows he kicked me everywhere else."

Bob, of course, was joking. Right, Bob? I'd hate to have to bring you out of retirement and get you back in the ring for a little more practice!

Actually, in Bob's book, *Priceless Memories,* he talks about how he learned karate from my brother Aaron and me. He tells of one time, after sparring with me one day and Aaron a few days later, his sides continuously ached from our kicks. So he went to the doctor for an X-ray. Barker writes, "The doctor said, 'You have two cracked ribs here and another two here.'"[2] Wow, I had no idea!

In all sincerity, my wife, Gena, and I send our love and congratulations to Bob for an incredibly successful career, in which he provided people around the world with lots of laughs, entertainment, and prizes. And I thank him for always being gracious to me, by crediting me with such words as these in an article in *Esquire* magazine: "I've done karate for thirty years. I studied with Chuck Norris. That's another reason I think I've lasted this long."[3]

"I hate that Bob Barker." > HAPPY GILMORE (ADAM SANDLER'S CHARACTER) IN THE MOVIE *HAPPY GILMORE*

 # CHUCK'S CODE (FIGHT)

It's relationships that matter in this life. Everything else is ultimately dust in the wind.

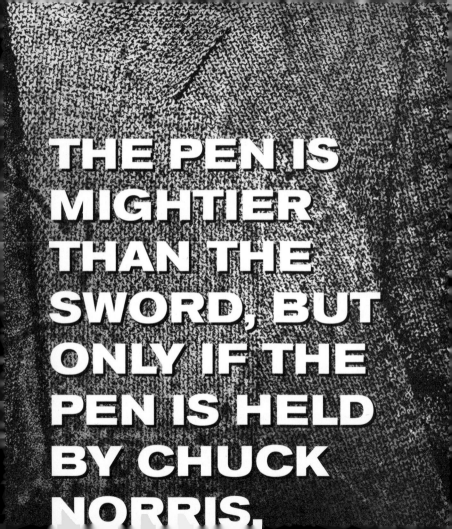

"Ask not what Chuck Norris can do for you. Ask what you can do for Chuck Norris."

LET'S BE HONEST . . .

America's founders definitely made the right choice when they created our republic.

It is interesting to note that on January 7, 1789, America's first presidential election was held. George Washington won the election and was sworn into office on April 30, 1789.

January 7? April 30? Probably not the dates you were expecting for a presidential election or inauguration, right?

It was not until 1845 that the Tuesday after the first Monday in November became the day that Americans appointed presidential electors in every fourth year. Moreover, it wasn't until 1875 that the date was established for electing U.S. Representatives in every even-numbered year. And it wasn't until 1914 that this date was used for electing U.S. Senators.

The unexpected happens a lot in life, even in politics. For better or worse, sometimes our candidates win; sometimes they lose. Sometimes our resolutions pass; sometimes they fail.

But one thing is certain: Without civic involvement, nothing in government would change. Nothing would improve. That's the system our Founding Fathers established—a government "of the people, by the people, and for the people."

Civic participation and service were not intended to be bottled up into one or two elections per year. If we expect our government to get back on track and truly represent us, then we've got to treat every calendar date just as importantly as election times. And never forget—*they* work for *us*; we don't work for them.

Don't like what you see in government? Tired of incumbent lethargy or inactivity? Does a political issue grind on you like fingernails on a chalkboard? It comes down to this: Either you will change the world or someone else will—but if you let someone else do it, you might not like his or her choices.

THEY SAID IT . . .

"As a rock star, I have two instincts: I want to have fun, and I want to change the world. I have a chance to do both." > BONO

CHUCK'S CODE (FREEDOM)

Either you will change the world or someone else will—but if you let someone else do it, you might not like his or her choices.

"Chuck Norris did in fact build Rome in a day."

LET'S BE HONEST . . .

Speaking of building a great society, there are some terrific stories about the influence of teenagers during the Revolutionary War. C. Brian Kelly's enjoyable work *Best Little Stories from the American Revolution* includes at least a few of them.

One in particular is about Marquis de Lafayette, who was only sixteen years old when he joined the Black Musketeers, an elite unit of royal troops that rode black horses.

After the Black Musketeers were disbanded in 1776, Lafayette volunteered to fight in the Revolutionary War. Congress granted the nineteen-year-old Frenchman the temporary rank of major general.

Lafayette became a favorite of George Washington's because he was rarely discouraged, always brave, and a true battlefield commander, unfazed by wounds or setbacks. He greatly aided General Washington and the success of the war. Two months after the British surrender at Yorktown, Lafayette returned home as a "hero of two worlds."

It's amazing for us today to think about how much a young Lafayette sacrificed and accomplished for our country and his own. We are still inspired by his example of youthful courage and heroism.

Many adults would say that type of valor rarely exists anymore. But as I meet and hear from young Americans here and around the world, I beg to differ. Though our society often denigrates the teen years and expects very little from our young people, I believe there exists a latent power in this particular generation that waits to be awakened and reveal its full potential.

Others might dismiss the potential of youth. Some might look down on young age. But the truth is, we all were born with a certain potential to make a difference in this life.

You were born with a purpose. You have a destiny. As my mother told me, "God has a plan for your life." Believe what God says about you. Live as if you believe it with your whole heart. And who knows? Someday you just might lead a revolution.

"Our uprising won't be marked by mass riots and violence, but by millions of individual teens quietly choosing to turn the low expectations of our culture upside down." > BRETT AND ALEX HARRIS[1]

CHUCK'S CODE (FREEDOM)

All life matters. All life has purpose. Man can be defeated but not destroyed. A defeat is simply that, and not the end of the world. Treat defeat as a temporary setback. Learn from it and try again with renewed vigor and determination.

OFFICIAL CHUCK
NORRIS FACT

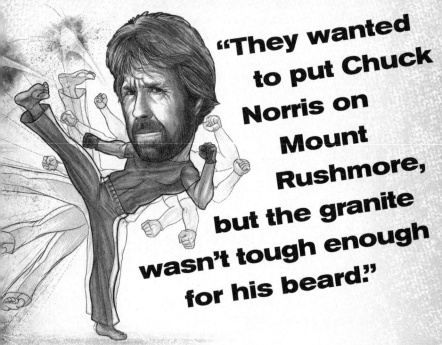

"They wanted to put Chuck Norris on Mount Rushmore, but the granite wasn't tough enough for his beard."

LET'S BE HONEST . . .

One of the geniuses of America's Founding Fathers was to provide and secure a foundation for our freedom of religious belief. The First Amendment simply reads, "Congress shall make no law respecting an establishment of religion, or prohibiting the free exercise thereof; or abridging the freedom of speech, or of the press; or the right of the people peaceably to assemble, and to petition the Government for a redress of grievances."

When Thomas Jefferson originally penned his legendary

commentary on the First Amendment—"a wall of separation between Church and State"—in his letter to the Danbury Baptists in 1802, he was concerned with prohibiting the domination and legislation of religious sectarianism in government, as it was back in England and even in some early colonies, such as Virginia. However, he was *not* trying to rid government of religious influence.[1]

That does not mean we enforce one religion on all people—that is what the First Amendment protects us from. I believe in the separation of religious sectarianism from government and protecting our religious institutions, such as churches, from the long arm of the federal government. I don't believe, however, in an erroneous interpretation of the Bill of Rights, or of Jefferson's and Madison's interpretive words, that would restrict religious or speech freedoms or produce a secular-progressive barrier that bans any religious influence in society.

Whatever your religious persuasion, don't be ashamed of it. This is America. And that's one of the things that still makes us a great nation. In God we trust.

THEY SAID IT . . .
"There! His Majesty can now read my name without glasses. And he can double the reward on my head!" > JOHN HANCOCK, AFTER SIGNING HIS NAME IN LARGE LETTERS ON THE DECLARATION OF INDEPENDENCE

CHUCK'S CODE (FAITH)

"In God We Trust—all others we search." A statement from my friend Dave LaGroue, who is a California Highway Patrolman.[2]

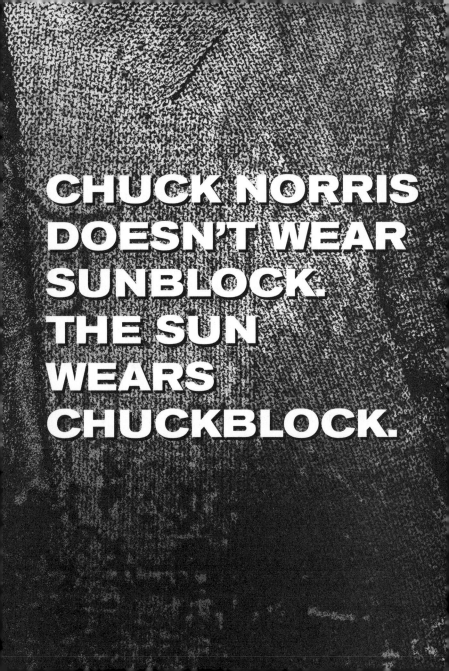

"Chuck Norris doesn't actually write books; the words assemble themselves out of fear."

LET'S BE HONEST . . .

I wish it were that easy!

Many people don't know that I've written six other books besides this one. I've written a book on America's culture wars, two Westerns, an autobiography (updated from a former version), and a self-help book of sorts:

Black Belt Patriotism: How to Reawaken America

Against All Odds: My Story (written with Ken Abraham)

A Threat to Justice: A Novel (with Ken Abraham, Aaron Norris, and Tim Grayem)

The Justice Riders: A Novel (with Ken Abraham, Aaron Norris, and Tim Grayem)

The Secret Power Within

The Secret of Inner Strength: My Story (with Joe Hyams)

I enjoy writing very much. It not only gives one a sense of contribution but also establishes a legacy for posterity's sake.

Though I've done some motivational speaking—hundreds of times over the past thirty years—I don't really like to speak in public. I'm willing, but my mouth doesn't always keep in step with my mind. That is one of the reasons I like the medium of writing. It allows me to think about what I want to say before putting it to pen.

Over the past couple of years, I've also written a weekly syndicated column for Creators Syndicate (www.creators.com) in Los Angeles, through which I stay engaged in America's culture wars on many fronts. It's been a wonderful venue for voicing my opinion on lots of issues.

My hope is to continue to write my weekly column and possibly one book a year. One should never quit striving to better oneself and contribute back to society.

THEY SAID IT . . .

"Books are the treasured wealth and the fit inheritance of generations and nations." > HENRY DAVID THOREAU

CHUCK'S CODE (FIGHT)

I will remain highly goal oriented throughout my life because that positive attitude helps family, my country, and me. (#12 of my Principles for Life)

OFFICIAL CHUCK
NORRIS FACT

"Nothing is certain in life except death, taxes, and a Chuck Norris roundhouse kick."

LET'S BE HONEST . . .

Actually, I'd like to make it so that only two of those elements are certain in life: death and a Chuck Norris roundhouse kick! If we implemented the Fair Tax, most other taxes would become obsolete.

The Fair Tax does away with all current taxes and puts in their place a single, fair tax on consumption, which is the closest practical and modern equivalent to the taxation system favored by America's founders. With the Fair Tax, the harder you work and the more money you make, the better off you *and* the American economy will be. You will pay taxes only when you buy something, which means that you can control how much you're taxed and you're never penalized for working hard.

As Mike Huckabee says, "Wouldn't it be nice if April 15 were just another sunny spring day?" It's time we had a system through which people didn't have to figure out ways to cheat in order to save their money. Again from Mike Huckabee:

> The Fair Tax is a completely transparent tax system. It doesn't increase taxes. It is revenue neutral. But here's what it will do. It will bring business back to the United States that [now] is leaving our shores because our tax laws make it impossible for an American-based business to compete. . . . The fair tax was designed by economists from Harvard and Stanford and some of the leading think tanks across the country.[1]

There are also trillions of American dollars hiding in offshore accounts. With the Fair Tax, the owners of this money can bring it back to invest in the United States, which would give a huge boost to our economy. It's the biggest stimulus package there is. Or, as the Fair Tax Web site says, "Think of it as the world's biggest economic jumper cables!"[2]

"Taxes on consumption are always least burdensome, because they are least felt, and are borne too by those who are both willing and able to pay them; that of all taxes on consumption, those on foreign commerce are most compatible with the genius and policy of Free States." > JAMES MADISON[3]

CHUCK'S CODE (FREEDOM)

When faced with a problem, don't worry about it. Worry is wasted energy. Get the job done the best way you can.

"There are no steroids in baseball, just players Chuck Norris has breathed on."

LET'S BE HONEST . . .

During my days as a fighter, I recognized the three facets of being a winner: mental, psychological, and physical.

I would prepare myself mentally by knowing my competitor's strengths and weaknesses and how I could take advantage of both. I would visualize myself fighting that particular opponent, defending myself against his strengths and attacking his weaknesses.

The difference between something vividly visualized and the actual experience is quite small. For example, imagine yourself walking down a dark alley. You see a place where someone could be hiding. You then imagine someone being there, and the hair on your head stands straight up. As you cautiously walk by, you then realize that no one was there, but your imagination worked as if there were. I won many fights using this technique.

I prepared myself psychologically by believing in my ability and being confident that I could win. I didn't always win—and it would surprise me when I didn't—but it didn't discourage me.

Last, I prepared myself physically by being in the best possible condition and being able to execute my techniques to the best of my ability. I knew that if I got physically tired, I might lose the will to win. When I was at the top of my form, I often hit an opponent before my brain could even record it.

There's an old adage I have always believed in: He who fails to prepare, prepares to fail. A winner says to himself, "*When* I win," not "*If* I win."

THEY SAID IT . . .

"Float like a butterfly, sting like a bee." > MUHAMMAD ALI

CHUCK'S CODE (FITNESS)

He who fails to prepare, prepares to fail.

"Chuck Norris can ride a motor without the cycle."

LET'S BE HONEST . . .

I smile inside when people tell me how lucky I've been. Believe me, luck had nothing to do with it. I succeeded by paying my dues in sweat, discipline, and years of hard work. I was never a natural athlete. I simply made up for what I lacked physically with drive and determination. I didn't just star in a movie; I personally marketed it from town to town around the country. I didn't just get lucky with 203 episodes of *Walker, Texas Ranger*; I worked fifteen hours a day, six days a week for nearly a decade. I didn't give up. I wouldn't allow myself to give up.

You've got to believe you can do that too. Believing in yourself is critical. Forget your past. Forget what you can't do. Start focusing on what you *can* do. You can truly do whatever you want, if you believe in your mind that you can achieve it. The secret to inner strength is belief and thinking positively.

For example, Bruce Lee had bad eyesight and one leg that was shorter than the other. But he had a mental image of what he wanted to achieve and who he wanted to be, and he became the quintessential martial artist and the first Chinese superstar in American film. Each step of his life was a progression toward his goal.

The wonderful thing about America is that you can start to succeed at any age, no matter where you came from. You might be from the Bronx, the prairies of Oklahoma, or the tip of Alaska—it doesn't matter. If you quit looking at your past as an obstacle to your future, and focus instead on the stepping-stones right in front of you—one at a time—you can create a new future.

I'm proof of it. Being successful is about hard work. Believe in yourself, be optimistic, and don't give up, no matter what.

THEY SAID IT . . .
"Building a better you is the first step to building a better America." > ZIG ZIGLAR

 CHUCK'S CODE (FITNESS)

Don't rely on luck—rather, focus on your goals,
be determined, and don't give up.

"Elvis never lived. He was just another manifestation of Chuck Norris."

LET'S BE HONEST . . .

That's hilarious. Elvis was born January 8, 1935. I was honored to know him and his wife, Priscilla. My first encounter with the Presleys, while Elvis and Priscilla were still married, was when she called to ask if she could take private lessons from me. I agreed and taught her at my martial arts studio in Sherman Oaks, California.

From her first lesson, Priscilla worked very hard. She was serious about her training. She learned quickly, in part because she had studied ballet, which gave her an edge over many students. She was already limber and able to execute high kicks with ease. Within a month, she was able to kick with force and precision anywhere I directed.

When we started freestyle sparring (a free exchange of blows, blocks, and counterattacks), I tried to get her to wear a boxer's head guard. Although most students welcomed the face protection, Priscilla rejected it. I'll never forget her response: "I won't have one of these on in the streets." Once she even insisted on going out in the alley behind the studio to work out on the asphalt in high-heel shoes because she said that was what she usually wore.

Priscilla has many of the qualities I value in a student. She is open and has a positive attitude toward life. She was a great example, even many years ago, of what we see very often today—women training and competing with the same diligence and fortitude as men. Ever since working with Priscilla, I've expected top results from both my male *and* female students. Today, women are often the fiercest competitors.

God has given us all potential to do good and great things—often exceeding what we think we are capable of. When's the last time you ventured out to try or learn something new? Stretch outside of your normal activity? Live outside the box? Until you try, you'll never know what is waiting—maybe even your black belt!

"Ambition is a dream with a V-8 engine." > ELVIS PRESLEY

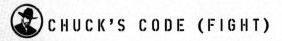

CHUCK'S CODE (FIGHT)

God has given us all potential to do good and great things—
often exceeding what we think we are capable of.

#60

OFFICIAL CHUCK
NORRIS FACT

"Chuck Norris fathered the Greatest Generation. That's why they were so tough."

LET'S BE HONEST . . .

In Tom Brokaw's book *The Greatest Generation*, he explains why the American generation who fought in World War II and rebuilt the postwar world deserves that title and our continued thanks:

☆ **162** ☆

They won the war; they saved the world. They came home to joyous and short-lived celebrations and immediately began the task of rebuilding their lives and the world they wanted. They married in record numbers and gave birth to another distinctive generation, the Baby Boomers. A grateful nation made it possible for more of them to attend college than any society had ever educated, anywhere. They gave the world new science, literature, art, industry, and economic strength unparalleled in the long curve of history.[1]

The Greatest Generation is a tough generation. I know because my mother, who is eighty-eight years old now, is a part of it. Like so many her age, she has lived with grace, optimism, and courage, despite facing some of life's greatest difficulties. She almost died at birth and again at ten years of age. She lived through the Great Depression and spent most of her life below the poverty level. She endured a perilous relationship with an alcoholic and mentally abusive husband (my father), who served in World War II and suffered irreparably from post-traumatic stress and the devil in the bottle. She single-handedly raised three boys, only to suffer the loss of her second son to the Vietnam War. She survived cancer, was a widow twice over, and has outlived all eight of her siblings.

What's amazing is that, through it all, I can't recall hearing Mom complain once. That is so typical of her generation, and they are to be commended for it.

My mother's generation, the Greatest Generation, deserves our thanks and praise. But they deserve more than that. They deserve our respect and remembrance for the America they built for us. We need to learn from their values and mimic their faithfulness.

We need to carry forward the America they handed to us, and not drop the baton and forget it in the sands of time.

I'm certain that if the Millennial Generation today could connect with the Greatest Generation of yesteryear, the America of tomorrow would be a better and brighter place.

THEY SAID IT . . .

"If I have seen further it is by standing on the shoulders of giants."
> ISAAC NEWTON[2]

 CHUCK'S CODE (FREEDOM)

Learn from and stand on the shoulders of your predecessors;
you'll see much further and find the future much brighter.

"Faster than a speeding bullet ... more powerful than a locomotive ... able to leap tall buildings in a single bound ... yes, these are some of Chuck Norris's warm-up exercises."

LET'S BE HONEST . . .

Exercise is very important to me. And here's exactly what I do to keep this thirty-nine-year-old body (with thirty years experience) in optimal condition. My wife, Gena, is my workout partner. I would suggest you get a workout partner who will help you stay motivated. Here is my weekly workout schedule:

Monday/Wednesday/Friday
Total Gym: I do a routine that takes me exactly fifteen minutes.

Fast Walk: Gena and I fast walk two miles or use one of our elliptical machines for thirty minutes.

Crunches: I do ten minutes of crunches for my abs.

Stretching: I finish with a few minutes of stretching.

Tuesday/Thursday/Saturday
Martial Arts: I start by stretching and then move on to isolated kicks in slow motion. Then I do hand-and-feet-combination strikes on a heavy bag. If I have someone to spar with, I practice my jujitsu.

Pool Exercise: Gena and I finish by doing kicks in the pool. Why do I use the pool? It has numerous benefits: Low-impact water workouts combine cardiovascular exercises with strength training, with little risk of injury. Even though you might feel lighter in the water, the added resistance makes the aerobics challenging. Water provides twelve times the resistance of air, because of its greater density. As water pushes against the body, the movements become more difficult, requiring muscles to work harder. I strongly recommend it.

THEY SAID IT . . .
"I tell people that I can't afford to die; it will wreck my image!"
> JACK LALANNE, FITNESS GURU

CHUCK'S CODE (FITNESS)

I don't want to oversimplify exercise, but it is basically whatever gets your heart pumping and uses major muscle groups. Physical employment, housework, playing with your kids, walking your dogs, working in the yard, dancing, biking, hiking, etc., are all good.

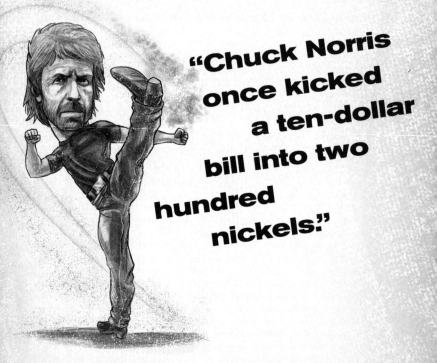

"Chuck Norris once kicked a ten-dollar bill into two hundred nickels."

LET'S BE HONEST . . .

If you're a twentysomething, it's likely you're facing a looming loan crisis. Not only has the cost of education skyrocketed, leaving many Millennials with more than fifty thousand dollars in student loans, but credit card companies have also devised new ways to ensure that your generation "remains friends" with consumer debt for life!

Recent research by Sallie Mae, a provider of student loans and college savings plans, discovered that the average undergraduate student had a balance of $3,173 in credit card debt in 2008—the highest balance in more than a decade of studies. More than one-fifth of undergraduates had balances between three thousand dollars and seven thousand dollars.[1]

And if you think that being older makes you less likely to incur debt, think again. According to financial advisor Dave Ramsey, 78 percent of Baby Boomers have accrued 59 percent of the total outstanding credit card debt.[2] The American Bankers Association says the average American family now carries eight thousand dollars of credit card debt.[3] Ninety-three percent of retirees carry some debt, and 30 percent of them say their debt is a problem. The average credit card debt for sixty-five- to sixty-nine-year-olds grew 217 percent over the last ten years to $5,844.[4]

With more than 640 million working credit cards in circulation (that's two for every American!), credit card companies are using new tactics, manipulation, and hidden charges in order to secure the cardholders for as long as they can.[5] Credit card companies are the Godzillas of greed, using deceptive methods of control and abuse that rival any slave-trafficking system. In 2006, the credit card industry "reaped a staggering $17.1 billion in controversial penalty fees alone—a tenfold rise in such fees in the last decade."[6]

Our Founding Fathers built this country to free us from tyranny. Tyranny comes in all different forms, including debt. Let us do all we can to financially free ourselves and others from the chains of debt bondage. As the Good Book encourages, "Let no debt remain outstanding, except the continuing debt to love one another."[7]

CHUCK'S CODE (FREEDOM)

Don't live beyond your means. Sometimes less is more.

"Chuck Norris is currently suing NBC, claiming that Law and Order are trademarked names for his left and right fists."

LET'S BE HONEST . . .

Before my film and television career, while I was ascending through the levels of martial arts championships, both my brothers, Aaron and Wieland, used to help me teach martial arts classes. We also used to go around and give exhibitions of our skills. And we allowed Aaron, our younger brother, to play the little brother who could beat up his older brothers with his "superior martial arts technique." People always enjoyed it and laughed hysterically to see Aaron take down his older brothers, especially the eldest one!

Wieland and Aaron went on to earn their black belts and became instructors in my schools.

Wieland and Aaron also served in the U.S. Army during the Vietnam War. Aaron served three years as a sergeant. Tragically, our brother Wieland never made it home from the war; he was killed in Vietnam.

Aaron was teaching martial arts at a studio in Virginia Beach when I was offered the starring role in *Good Guys Wear Black*. I called Aaron and told him I needed him as my stunt coordinator on the film, which he agreed to do. After that film, Aaron continued to stunt coordinate and second-unit direct all my films, such as *A Force of One*, *The Octagon*, and *Lone Wolf McQuade*, until we did *Braddock: Missing in Action III* and I asked Aaron to direct that film. He did such an incredible job directing that I asked him to direct six more of my films.

After a couple of seasons of the *Walker, Texas Ranger* series, when I desperately needed some help, I asked Aaron to come on as my co-executive producer. He did, and the show started running more smoothly, generating even higher ratings, and becoming less stressful for me. Aaron has been my right arm in my film and TV career. Without him, I'm not sure if I would have had the success I was blessed with.

I SAID IT . . .

"I've always admired you, little brother. We've been through thick and thin together, and here we are still standing today. What a ride! I have always considered you to be one of my best friends and one of the greatest blessings God has given me in this life. I love you, Aaron—always have, always will. > LOVE, YOUR BROTHER, CARLOS"

CHUCK'S CODE (FAMILY)

Never be afraid to say, "I love you." Those are three powerful words that should be spoken often.

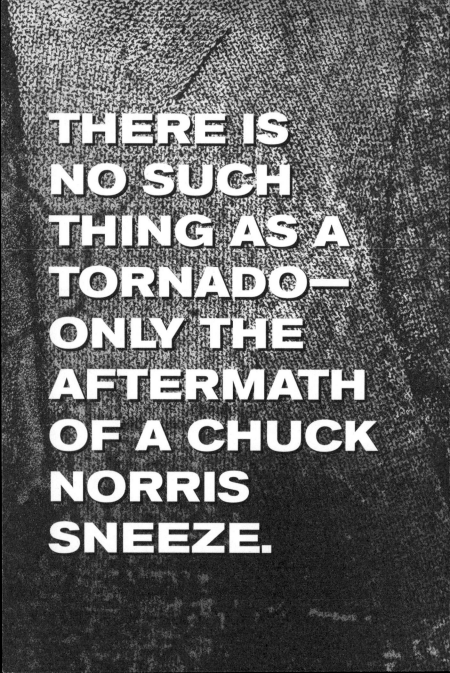

THERE IS NO SUCH THING AS A TORNADO—ONLY THE AFTERMATH OF A CHUCK NORRIS SNEEZE.

"Chuck Norris can taste lies."

LET'S BE HONEST . . .

I was raised on the Ten Commandments and the Golden Rule:
Do unto others as you would have them do unto you. They are
principles I've always believed should be at the heart of America
and Americans' lives.

The founders of our country had three documents that

should be on the walls of each of our homes: the Constitution, the Declaration of Independence, and the Ten Commandments. For the founders, the Ten Commandments represented a foundation for morality and civility.

Many people may not know that each of the original thirteen colonies codified into law every one of the Ten Commandments, which then served as a basis for their ethics and conduct.[1] And the preambles of most of the states' original constitutions contain an acknowledgment to Almighty God or a Supreme Ruler.[2]

Noah Webster, the author and publisher of America's first dictionary, explained two centuries ago, "The duties of men are summarily comprised in the Ten Commandments, consisting of two tables; one comprehending the duties which we owe immediately to God—the other, the duties we owe to our fellow men." John Witherspoon, a signer of the Declaration of Independence, president of Princeton, and a legislator who served on more than one hundred committees while in Congress, declared, "The Ten Commandments . . . are the sum of the moral law."

This is how America's founders strengthened morality and encouraged civility across our great land—and how we can today as well.

USA Today recently reported on a new study out of Harvard University, which revealed that people of faith make better citizens and better neighbors.[3] The study says that religious people are three to four times more likely to be involved in their community. They are more prone than nonreligious Americans to work on community projects, attend public meetings, belong to voluntary associations, attend protest demonstrations and political rallies, vote in local elections, and donate time, talents, and treasures to causes, including secular ones.

"The Law given from Sinai [the Ten Commandments] was a civil and municipal as well as a moral and religious code."

> JOHN QUINCY ADAMS, SIXTH U.S. PRESIDENT, WRITING TO HIS SON

CHUCK'S CODE (FAITH)

Moral absolutes strengthen morals absolutely.

"If you were somehow able to land a punch on Chuck Norris, your entire arm would shatter on impact."

(This is only a theory, because who in their right mind would even try this?)

LET'S BE HONEST . . .

People ask me all the time, "Do you still teach the martial arts?"
I don't personally, but I still train, and I have equipped many other
leaders through the years who in turn train others, and on and on
it goes. Through my **KICKSTART KIDS** program and my United
Fighting Arts Federation (UFAF), I'm proud to say that we have
promoted more than 2,300 black belts all over the world.[1]

My system of martial arts is called Chun Kuk Do, in which

all my black belts (UFAF members) train. *Chun Kuk Do* means "universal way," which represents a unification of many different systems—jujitsu, judo, karate, Tae Kwon Do—all merged into one. Over the fifty years that I've been training, I've trained in almost every martial arts style there is, and I've blended them all together in what I believe is one of the finest forms of self-defense.

UFAF is the governing and sanctioning body for my Chun Kuk Do martial arts style, providing technical standards for instruction and advancement in the system. UFAF is a membership organization that provides its member students, instructors, and schools with Chun Kuk Do rank certification, educational opportunities, special events, online community access, and other services. Black belts in Chun Kuk Do receive certification of their rank from me personally.

If you're interested in learning Chun Kuk Do from one of our schools, you can locate a local academy by going to the UFAF Web site.[2] Also, every July, UFAF members and others are invited to Las Vegas for our Chun Kuk Do International Training Conference and World Championships.

THEY SAID IT . . .

"I refer to my hands, feet, and body as the tools of the trade. The hands and feet must be sharpened and improved daily to be efficient." > BRUCE LEE

 CHUCK'S CODE (FIGHT)

Be a perpetual student. It's what you learn after you know it all that counts.

"Similar to a Russian nesting doll, if you were to break Chuck Norris open, you would find another Chuck Norris inside—only smaller and tougher."

LET'S BE HONEST . . .

When I was growing up, my family was very poor. Because of my alcoholic father's irresponsibility, we lived in several places, including Oklahoma, California, and Arizona. But Mom and God provided all the security we ultimately needed.

I used to patrol the streets of Wilson, Oklahoma, every day after school and collect soda bottles that I would return to the grocer for a refund. I also picked up scrap iron that I sold for a penny a pound.

There was one movie theater in Wilson where, for a dime, I could spend all Saturday afternoon watching the double feature and the serials. I loved those Saturdays. With a nickel bag of popcorn on my lap, I could escape into another world. I went to Casablanca with Humphrey Bogart, and Cary Grant took me to India. My favorite movies were Westerns, especially ones with John Wayne. For those few hours in the movie theater when I was watching a John Wayne movie, I *became* him.

Like many kids at that age, I dreamed of becoming a cowboy. I remember seeing a toy gun in a store window and wanting it more than anything else in the world. But my mother couldn't afford it. It was a big disappointment to me, and she knew it, but she said there would be many things in life that I would not be able to have when I wanted them, and I should think of them as goals to be achieved. If I kept the goal in mind, accepting the fact that there would be setbacks and obstacles, and continued to work toward succeeding, one day I would reach that goal. That was pretty heady stuff for a kid to understand, but some of it sank in. Much, much later, it became an integral part of my own life philosophy.

Although I grew up amid poverty and dysfunction, my mother established all the right groundwork in my life, from a Christian faith to a hard work ethic. But it would take decades for me to really understand the power of what she had done for my brothers and me.

"If you ever start feeling like you have the goofiest, craziest, most dysfunctional family in the world, all you have to do is go to a state fair. [After] five minutes at the fair, you'll be going, 'You know, we're all right.'" > JEFF FOXWORTHY

CHUCK'S CODE (FAMILY)

Every family tree has nuts. Get over it.

---

and their families to many of my movie and television sets, giving them hope, strength, and joy to endure difficult times.

This past year, we heard about a 13-year-old young man named Nickolas (Nick) Yancy Nischan, in Kentucky, who gave up his wish to meet me so that his family could take a vacation and experience a little relief and comfort from the hardships of watching him suffer. As he had done many times before, Nick sacrificed his own desires and instead asked for a wish that would bless his family.

When Gena and I heard about this, we wanted to fulfill his wish, but because of other pre scheduled events, we were unable to visit Nick in person. What we were able to do was put together a video at my Texas ranch, in which my family, my friends, and I were able to offer Nick and his family some words of encouragement while giving them a tour of our oak-tree-filled prairie during a Texas sunset.

Before sending the video, which was tied to Steven Curtis Chapman's inspirational song "God Is God," we prayed for Nick and his family. We heard that he watched it over and over and over before he passed away. Nick truly exemplified the courage in death that he did in life, summarized by his favorite Bible verse: "Have I not commanded you? Be strong and courageous! Do not tremble or be dismayed, for the Lord your God is with you wherever you go."[1]

Nick is in heaven now—a place that the Bible describes as having "no more death or mourning or crying or pain."[2] I believe that's the life Nick experiences right now. And I believe he even frequently laughs, especially when he thinks about one of the lighter moments in that earthly video we made for him.

It was a moment in which I presented him with a T-shirt that had on the front the following Chuck Norris Fact: "When Chuck Norris does push-ups, he isn't lifting himself up; he's pushing the earth down."

OFFICIAL CHUCK
NORRIS FACT #67

"When Chuck Norris does push-ups, he isn't lifting himself up; he's pushing the earth down."

LET'S BE HONEST . . .

Gena and I have been honored to assist the Make-A-Wish
Foundation numerous times over the years by helping to fulfill t
wishes of children with life-threatening medical conditions. The
nation's largest wish-granting organization has brought childre

☆ 18

Immediately after reading the Fact aloud to Nick, a friend interjected, "Chuck, can we see you do that right now?"

I thought for a moment and then looked into the camera and asked, "Would you like to see me do that, Nick?" I then fell forward to the ground and started doing push-ups.

Before I sent the DVD to Nick and his family, I had a film editor insert scenes of people losing their footing in an earthquake and the earth moving up and down in space! (If you'd like to see the thirty-second segment in which I push the earth down, Nick's family has granted us permission to post that small clip on YouTube in Nick's honor. You can find it in a search under "Chuck Norris pushing the earth down.")

There's obviously nothing funny about children with life-threatening medical conditions. But most of us realize that, even in life's darkest moments, there's a place to lighten someone's spirit with a little respectful humor. From what I know about Nick, he kept the world smiling and even laughing throughout his six-and-a-half year fight with cancer.[3]

THEY SAID IT . . .

"Life does not cease to be funny when someone dies, any more than it ceases to be serious when someone laughs."

> GEORGE BERNARD SHAW[4]

CHUCK'S CODE (FREEDOM)

When it comes to the passing of those you love, laugh when you can, cry when you must, and don't ever forget to remember.

OFFICIAL CHUCK
NORRIS FACT

"Scientific fact: Roundhouse kicks are comprised primarily of an element called Chucktonium."

LET'S BE HONEST . . .

Growing up, I wanted to be a police officer. When I finished high school, I thought, *Okay, I'm eighteen years old. I can't join the police department, so I'll join the military for four years and get some police experience in the military.*

So I joined the Air Force and became an MP—military policeman. I was sent to Korea, where I thought, *Maybe I should learn judo.* (I hadn't heard of karate or Tae Kwon Do at the time.) So I enrolled in a judo class. But only two weeks into my training, I broke my shoulder.

☆ **186** ☆

Not being able to train with a sling on my arm, I decided to go sightseeing in a nearby village. As I walked along, I looked up to a knoll and saw heads popping up. I was curious, so I walked to the top of the knoll. On the other side, I saw several Koreans jumping in the air and doing spinning heel kicks and other moves. I said, "Holy mackerel! I didn't think the human body could do something like that."

I was mesmerized by their incredible ability. I wanted to ask them what they were doing, but they looked very intense. So I returned to the base and described what I had seen to my judo instructor, Master Ahn. He said it was called Tang Soo Do. I told him that I'd love to try it, since I couldn't do judo with my injured shoulder. He took me to the village and introduced me to Master Lee, who became my first instructor. I then discovered that Master Shin was teaching Tang Soo Do on base. I thought it would be easier to train there than to travel to the village, so I began training with Master Shin. I trained Monday through Saturday in Tang Soo Do and judo on Sundays.

By the time I left Korea, I had earned my black belt in Tang Soo Do and my brown belt in judo.

THEY SAID IT . . .

"A journey of a thousand miles must begin with a single step."

> LAO-TZU

CHUCK'S CODE (FIGHT)

A combination of discipline and learning leads to confidence. Remember that everyone is a beginner at some point in his or her life; even your teacher was once a pupil.

#69 OFFICIAL CHUCK
NORRIS FACT

"What is the last thing you hear before Chuck Norris gives you a roundhouse kick? No one knows, because dead men tell no tales."

LET'S BE HONEST . . .

Two years ago, *Parade* magazine conducted an online poll, asking the question, "Who would you rate as the toughest martial arts star ever on the big screen?"[1]

America was given five choices: the late Bruce Lee, Jet Li, Steven Seagal, Jean-Claude Van Damme, and me. I was humbly honored to be voted number one.

Truth be known, however, each of these men is an equally valiant warrior in his own right. And, of course, movies are quite different from real life. Fighting in the ring is definitely much more difficult than brawling in front of the camera. (I always preferred the open cuts and broken bones on film!)

Today, there are many superb martial artists and action figures, on and off the big screen. Who doesn't enjoy watching the speed and flexibility of martial artists such as Jet Li and Jackie Chan? Equally entertaining are the strong-arm heroine actresses such as Michelle Yeoh, Famke Janssen, Uma Thurman, Milla Jovovich, and Lucy Liu.

I'm grateful that action figures—and particularly martial artists—continue to influence and entertain on the big screen. Long gone are the days when Bruce Lee and I "fought to the death" in the Colosseum. But present and coming are a new group of actors who will keep the action arena alive and well.

Long live the martial arts in movies!

THEY SAID IT . . .

"Size matters not. . . . Look at me. Judge me by my size, do you?"

> YODA IN *STAR WARS: EPISODE V–THE EMPIRE STRIKES BACK*

CHUCK'S CODE (FIGHT)

Surpassing another person should not be your goal. The only thing that really matters is what you accomplish yourself.

"Chuck Norris doesn't need a weapon— he is one."

(Found on a Porta Potti in Al Asad, Iraq)

LET'S BE HONEST . . .

When I visited our troops in the Middle East for the second time in 2007, I was honored to shake hands with nearly twenty thousand troops at fifteen bases around Iraq. One of the other great joys of the trip was being able to meet the Iraqi people and those being trained for the Iraqi army and police. How wonderful it was to see their smiles and hear their stories—through an interpreter, of course.

On one occasion, at an Iraqi training area, one of the officers began to speak in Arabic to me. As he spoke, he smiled and held up his hand to his mouth, biting the air as if he were inviting us to dinner. An interpreter came over, started listening, and then smiled and told us what the Iraqi officer was trying to convey to me.

"'In the movie *Missing in Action 2*,' he wants to know, 'was that a real rat you had in your mouth?'"

"It was a real rat," I said.

We all began to laugh hysterically when we saw the surprised look on the Iraqi officer's face. I was equally amazed that he had even seen the movie!

It might seem like a trite story in the midst of a troubling war, but it really had an impact on me. Here we were, a group of Americans and Iraqis smiling, sharing stories, and laughing together. It gave me hope.

Call me overly optimistic, but I believe that better days are coming for America and the world. I believe we can move away from being world-peace officers (keeping a lid on things by force) to being instruments of world peace (modeling how to live in freedom, harmony, and peace, despite our differences). It doesn't start with our elected officials. It starts when we are willing to cross cultures (even in our own neighborhoods), extend a hand of peace, and maybe even share a story that brings a smile or laugh to others.

THEY SAID IT . . .

"If we have no peace, it is because we have forgotten that we belong to each other." > MOTHER TERESA

CHUCK'S CODE (FREEDOM)

Never lose hope. At the end of every storm the sun will shine again.

"Scientists have estimated that the energy given off during the Big Bang was roughly equal to 1 CNRK: One Chuck Norris Roundhouse Kick."

LET'S BE HONEST . . .

Like me, my brothers, Wieland and Aaron, were patriots. At the height of the Vietnam War, they both enlisted in the U.S. Army. Aaron was stationed in Korea, and Wieland was sent to Vietnam. As my little brother headed off to Nam, I hugged and kissed him and said, "I'm going to miss you. Be careful."

I was refereeing a martial arts tournament in California one day when I heard an announcement over the loudspeaker: "Chuck Norris, you have an urgent call."

When I picked up the phone, I recognized the muffled voice of my mother-in-law, and she was crying. She said, "Wieland has been killed in Vietnam."

If I had been kicked in the stomach by a dozen karate champions at the same time, it could not have affected me more. I staggered away from the phone, as if that would somehow make the words untrue. No family should have to feel what my mother; my other brother, Aaron; and I felt that day. And yet so many do, every day, every year.

I hung up the phone, moving in what felt like slow motion. For a long time, I couldn't function. I simply sat in shock, thinking about my little brother, my best friend, whom I would never see again in this life. Right there, in front of anyone who cared to see, I wept uncontrollably.

When Wieland was twelve years old, he had a premonition that he would not live to be twenty-eight. He died on June 3, 1970, one month before his twenty-eighth birthday.

It is fitting for a soldier like Wieland that every year Memorial Day falls a week or so before the anniversary of the day when he gave his life in service to his country. It was to Wieland that I dedicated all my *Missing in Action* films.

THEY SAID IT . . .

"There is no greater love than to lay down one's life for one's friends." > JESUS (JOHN 15:13, NLT)

CHUCK'S CODE (FAMILY)

Sacrifice is never in vain. It is valued into eternity.

☆ **195** ☆

#72

OFFICIAL CHUCK
NORRIS FACT

"Giraffes were created when Chuck Norris uppercut a horse."

LET'S BE HONEST . . .

This Fact is particularly hilarious and poignant to me, because I live on a ranch with horses and cattle. What a funny word picture!

Gena and I believe in preserving rural America and the core values and principles on which our country was founded. The educational philosophy of America's founders gave priority to teaching on morality and religion, including the Bible. Benjamin Rush, a signer of the Declaration of Independence, wrote to the citizens of Philadelphia in *A Plan for Free Schools* in 1787, "Let the children who are sent to those schools be taught to read and write. . . . Above all, let both sexes be carefully instructed in the principles and obligations of the Christian religion. This is the most essential part of education."

Noah Webster, "the Father of American Scholarship and Education," stated, "In my view, the Christian religion is the most important and one of the first things in which all children, under a free government, ought to be instructed. . . . No truth is more evident to my mind than that the Christian religion must be the basis of any government intended to secure the rights and privileges of a free people."

In 1789, around the same time when the First Amendment to the Constitution was written, guaranteeing freedom of religion, President George Washington signed into law the Northwest Ordinance, which states, "Religion, morality, and knowledge, being necessary to good government and the happiness of mankind, schools, and the means of education shall forever be encouraged."

That is why Gena and I are on the board of the National Council on Bible Curriculum in Public Schools, which is helping our schools implement an elective course on the Bible as history and literature. Roughly 478 public school districts and 1,975 high schools in thirty-eight states are offering a course on it, and 353,600 students have already been taught from it. You, too, can learn more about the curriculum, why its teaching is constitutional, and how it can be implemented in your public schools. Contact them:

National Council on Bible Curriculum in Public Schools
PO Box 9743
Greensboro, NC 27429
1-877-On-Bible or 1-336-272-3799
www.bibleinschools.net

THEY SAID IT . . .
"God, the source of all knowledge, should never have been
expelled from our children's classrooms." > RONALD REAGAN,
ADDRESS TO NATIONAL RELIGIOUS BROADCASTERS, WASHINGTON, D.C.,
JANUARY 1984

 CHUCK'S CODE (FAITH)

Be educated, not indoctrinated.
Don't be afraid to examine the options.

"Chuck Norris was 'Made in the USA'— Using Steel and Alloys."

LET'S BE HONEST . . .

Most Americans will try to justify their purchasing of foreign goods. And many of their reasons—ranging from availability to price to quality—make perfect sense. But as we learned in recent months when gas prices went through the roof, we enable foreign dominance in commerce—and perhaps in other areas of life as well—when we simply pay the price and don't come up with other alternatives.

We say we "can't afford" to buy American—but maybe it's time to say we can't afford not to.[1] By supporting our homeland industries, we not only invest in America and boost our economy, but we also help to reverse the staggering unemployment rates and keep our companies from going under. We all can do our part to keep America strong by buying American goods and services.

But be careful with labels. There's an obvious difference between "Made in the USA" and "Assembled in the USA." Some labels are misleading, so do your homework. Take some time to understand what it means for a business to comply with the "Made in the USA" standards.[2] Check reputable consumer Web sites to search for domestic manufactured goods and services.[3]

According to a Gallup poll, the good news is that 72 percent of Americans today are more concerned with the geographical origin of products they purchase, and most are willing to pay more for American-made products.[4] For many, "Made in the USA" labels represent an increased concern for work and environmental conditions, as well as premium quality and consumer safety.[5] Buying American is also a way to rekindle patriotism.

Remember when "Made in the USA" was a badge of honor? Well, I'm proposing a buyers' revolution in which we all economically win that medal of valor. If the government isn't going to help us by securing our borders, reducing the outsourcing, ceasing debt through bogus bailouts and out-of-control spending, then "We the People" must take back the financial future of our nation. Let's make sure that *the buck stops here*—in America. That is one resolution we all should make over the next year: Buy "Made in the USA."

Don't just *go* green; *spend* green—on American-made products and services. If just half of the country followed suit, our down-turned economy would turn on a dime.

THEY SAID IT . . .
"Do you guys have to sell everything? . . . I'd like to buy the Earth's core." > JON STEWART IN AN INTERVIEW WITH AMAZON.COM[6]

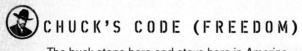

CHUCK'S CODE (FREEDOM)

The buck stops here and stays here in America.
Buy "Made in the USA."

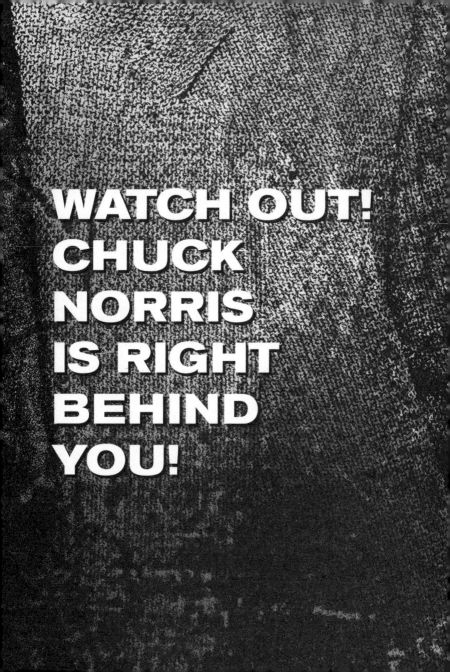

"Chuck Norris can play a guitar without the strings."

(And we're not talking about Guitar Hero!)

LET'S BE HONEST . . .

A couple of years into filming the *Walker, Texas Ranger* series, I received a song from a country singer-songwriter from Oklahoma City. The song was called "The Eyes of a Ranger." I read the lyrics and saw that he had captured what the show was all about. I bought the rights to the song, and my next thought was to get my friend Randy Travis to sing the song.

I sent the song to CBS, saying, "I've found the perfect song that should be the theme song for *Walker*, and I'd like to get Randy Travis to sing it."

CBS responded, "We like the song, but we think you should sing it."

"Me? I'm not a singer!"

CBS replied, "You sing it, or else we don't use it."

Now, most actors have a secret desire to sing, and many singers have a secret desire to act—and I'm no different. So I said, "Okay, let me go into the recording studio and see what I can do."

I went to a sound studio in LA to attempt to record the song. The instrumental background music had already been recorded, so all I had to do was sing my vocals. *How hard could that be?*

I sounded awful, but the producer and engineer were very encouraging and patient with me. It took nearly twelve hours to record my vocals; but thanks to the miracles of modern recording technology, the song didn't sound half bad.

There were portions of the song in which I had to speak the lyrics, similar to what Johnny Cash did on many of his songs. There was simply no way I could sing them. I guess you could call me a "Country Rapper"!

And that's how "The Eyes of a Ranger" became the theme song for *Walker, Texas Ranger*.

THEY SAID IT . . .

"When you think about the fact that we were on Late Night for sixteen years, closing in on three thousand shows, I feel like if we don't change, we're going to be in trouble. It's like saying to the Beatles, 'Don't change your mop tops. Keep singing "I Wanna Hold Your Hand."' There, I've just compared myself to the Beatles."

> CONAN O'BRIEN, CREATOR OF THE *WALKER, TEXAS RANGER* LEVER[1]

CHUCK'S CODE (FIGHT)

We're creatures of comfort, but life is an adventure.
Don't be afraid to go outside the box.

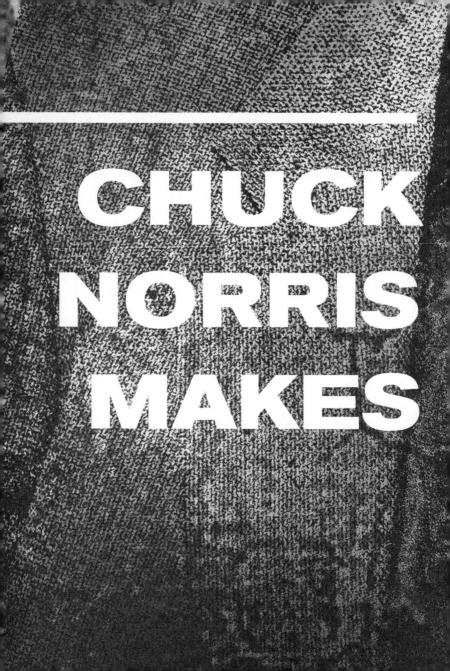

ONIONS CRY.

#75 OFFICIAL CHUCK NORRIS FACT

"Chuck Norris can unscramble an egg."

LET'S BE HONEST . . .

At the heart of the culture wars is the most easily overlooked battle of all, because it's literally right before our eyes (at least three times a day). I call it the consumption war. Its ultimate goal is to control us as much as any other facet of the culture war—to win us over to its ways. Sadly, it appears to be working in too many American homes and restaurants.

Our culture is entrenched in hedonism, which means that all we care about is pleasure. We go where we feel like going. We do what we feel like doing. We watch what we feel like watching. And we eat what we feel like eating. And God help the soul who tells us to do otherwise.

The problem is that we're literally killing ourselves in the pleasure process. Like putting bad gasoline in a car, bad food contributes to bad health. (We've also heard people say that they want to retire early, but have you ever heard anyone say they want to die early?) And that is exactly what many people are doing—which is why Mike Huckabee says, "We're digging our graves with a knife and fork."[1]

The problem is that we've confused liberty with licentiousness. We think doing what we feel like doing is power and freedom, when really it's just carrying out what our flesh craves. True freedom is being able to look straight in the eye of what you feel like doing and possessing the power to do otherwise. Eating anything we want isn't liberty—it's tyranny. Eating what is right is freedom— it's victory over oppression. Triumph over the tummy is another ongoing goal we should have in this life. Fighting for a better America includes fighting for a healthier, fitter, combat-ready you.

You can't fight a culture war if you're dead. That sounds a bit extreme, but it's true. Any collection of challenges from me must include an encouragement to be healthy. I want you to live as optimally as you can, with all the gusto your life can experience and offer.

THEY SAID IT . . .
"The way to any man or woman's heart, or any other part of their anatomy, is through their stomach." > RACHAEL RAY

CHUCK'S CODE (FITNESS)

Fight against a culture of apathy and unhealthiness.

**OFFICIAL CHUCK
NORRIS FACT**

"Nothing can escape the gravity of a black hole, except for Chuck Norris. Chuck Norris eats black holes. They taste like chicken."

LET'S BE HONEST . . .

As a young man, I indulged in fast foods, snacks, and occasional malts. But when I was in my thirties, I realized that I had to become more aware of what I put into my body. Education and awareness made a major difference, both physically and mentally.

You might be young, but no one is immune to bad health. There are, however, ways to build up your body and immunities so that you stay fit even as you age.

According to the World Health Organization and the Centers for Disease Control and Prevention, childhood and teen obesity in the United States has tripled over the last thirty years. Twenty-five percent of kids are overweight or obese, and most parents don't even know it.[1] They also report one-third of adults are now overweight, with another third being obese. According to their data, those numbers have "increased sharply for both adults and children" since the 1970s.[2]

But if eating and obesity exacerbate illnesses and mortality statistics, the good news is that they are also the most preventable causes of death in America. Of course, genetics, environment, socioeconomic status, metabolism, and behavior can be contributors to these ailments; but the fact is that most Americans are overweight because they eat poorly and don't exercise. Many of the processed foods we eat are high in fat, sugar, and salt. And compared to other countries, we eat much larger portions.

To keep yourself in optimal condition, I recommend good and encouraging nutritional reading, such as Dr. Tedd Mitchell's book *Move Yourself,* and Dr. Don Colbert's book *Seven Pillars of Health.*[3] Dr. Colbert gives an excellent treatise about the seven cores of every healthy life and soul. What I love about his approach and materials is that he simplifies complex matters and boils down the web of a healthy lifestyle into seven simple steps:

1. Drink sufficient amounts of water.
2. Get adequate amounts of sleep.
3. Eat living foods.

4. Regularly exercise or "stir the waters."
5. Detoxify your body.
6. Take adequate amounts of nutritional supplements.
7. Reduce stress.

To that list of seven, I would add an eighth step: Feed yourself spiritually.

Be good to your body, even at a young age; otherwise you might not live to experience everything you want to. Or as sisters Bessie and Sadie Delany recommended a few years before they died (Bessie at 104 and Sadie at 109): "God gave you only one body, so you better be nice to it. Exercise, because if you don't, by the time you're our age, you'll be pushing up daisies."

THEY SAID IT . . .

"You can't help getting older, but you don't have to get old."

> COMEDIAN GEORGE BURNS, WHO LIVED TO BE 100

 CHUCK'S CODE (FITNESS)

Everything in moderation.

"Chuck Norris can slam a revolving door.

LET'S BE HONEST . . .

It has been said that if God closes a door, he'll open a window. I've found that to be true over and over, not only in my life but in the lives of others as well.

After I was discharged from the military, I started teaching the martial arts in Torrance, California, in 1962. I wasn't sure where to find students because no one knew anything about the martial arts at that time.

When competitions in the United States started in 1963, I decided to enter, hoping I would get a write-up in the local paper. My first competition was in Salt Lake City, Utah. I drove all the way from Torrance with three of my students.

I had very little money and an old car, and we barely made it to Salt Lake City. All four of us competed, and my three students won their divisions. I lost mine. They held their trophies while I drove us back to California.

As I kept losing, I developed a philosophy. Each time I lost, I told myself, *I may lose again, but I won't lose the same way twice*. I just kept learning from my mistakes and finally started a winning streak. Eventually, I became the number one competitor in the United States. In 1968, I won the world middleweight karate championship at Madison Square Garden in New York City.

My motivation for becoming a competitor was to get students to attend my school. I knew how the martial arts had helped me, and I wanted to help my students. My motivation for starting the **KICKSTART KIDS** program was exactly the same: to give kids the opportunities to learn discipline and to build their self-esteem.

THEY SAID IT . . .

"In strategy, it is important to see distant things as if they were close and to take a distanced view of close things." > MIYAMOTO MUSASHI, 1584–1645, LEGENDARY JAPANESE SWORDSMAN

CHUCK'S CODE (FIGHT)

Learn from your losses. Don't lose the same way twice.

"Chuck Norris can hear the silence."

LET'S BE HONEST . . .

One of the wisest decisions of America's Founding Fathers was to provide and secure the firm foundation in the First Amendment: "Congress shall make no law respecting an establishment of religion, or prohibiting the free exercise thereof; or abridging the freedom of speech, or of the press; or the right of the people peaceably to assemble, and to petition the government for a redress of grievances."

I remember several years ago watching Diane Sawyer interview Saddam Hussein on *20/20*. She respectfully confronted him about atrocities and executions he had authorized as punishment for people who merely spoke a word against him, his rule, or his politics. Surprisingly naive of America's constitutional basis, Saddam asked, "Well, what happens to those who speak against your president?" (From the tone of his question, he was clearly expecting that such speech was also a crime in the United States and punishable by law.)

Taken aback by Saddam's ignorance of the United States, and somewhat at a loss for words herself, Ms. Sawyer quipped, "They host television talk shows!" Saddam's facial expression revealed that he was totally confused by her answer.

Offensive speech being punishable by law? It sounds far-out, doesn't it? But it might not be that far away for America, especially if the course of free speech continues on its present track—a path of progressive restrictions, both from our government and our culture through social pressures.

It's simply un-American and unconstitutional to impede, harass, threaten, or persecute anyone who is guilty of nothing more than sharing his or her opinion or even exercising the right to vote. But when free speech is restricted or persecuted, we can be certain that we've drifted from our constitutional roots. This is America—not Saddam's Iraq. And if the First Amendment is not there to also protect someone's politically incorrect or offensive speech, then what type of speech does it protect?

Our founders would want us to remember what they established—a nation free from tyranny and oppression. Thomas Jefferson was particularly passionate and eloquent on this point: "I have sworn upon the altar of God eternal hostility against every form of tyranny over the mind of man."[1] These words are indelibly inscribed on the Jefferson Memorial in Washington, D.C. They apply equally to the dominance of religious sectarianism and the prohibition of free speech.

THEY SAID IT . . .

"History will have to record that the greatest tragedy of this period of social transition was not the strident clamor of the bad people, but the appalling silence of the good people."

> MARTIN LUTHER KING JR.

CHUCK'S CODE (FREEDOM)

Don't just respect other people's free speech; fight for it.

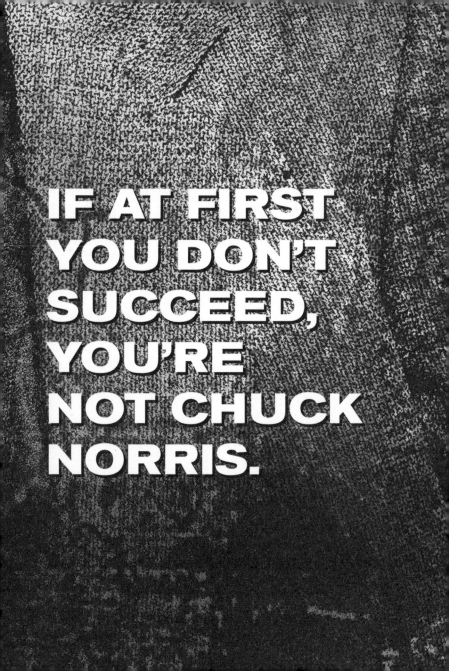

"Chuck Norris knows when you are sleeping. He knows when you're awake. He knows if you've been bad or good. So play dead for goodness' sake."

LET'S BE HONEST . . .

In veteran researcher and sociologist George Barna's new book, *The Seven Faith Tribes*, he indicates that the United States has seven dominant faith tribes that hold the key to the restoration of the nation.[1] Barna says, "Our faith tribes are central to the development and application of people's worldviews, which in turn produce the values on which we base our daily decisions." He further explains, "America cannot return to greatness simply by addressing its current financial challenges. . . . It is up to our faith tribes to demonstrate the courageous leadership necessary to facilitate a national restoration of the mind, heart, and soul."[2]

Barna agrees with America's founders about the preeminence of religion in society. While establishing the First Amendment right to freely embrace religion of choice, the founders depended on a Creator and religion (not the government or even education) to establish morality and civility in individuals and society.[3] That is why John Adams wrote, "Our Constitution was made only for a moral and religious people. It is wholly inadequate to the government of any other."

George Washington challenged Americans in his presidential farewell address: "Of all the dispositions and habits which lead to political prosperity, religion and morality are indispensable supports. . . . Whatever may be conceded to the influence of refined education on minds of peculiar structure, reason and experience both forbid us to expect that national morality can prevail in exclusion of religious principle."[4]

I respect all religions, and I encourage people not to be ashamed of their beliefs. That is why I balance my belief by agreeing with Benjamin Rush, a signer of the Declaration of Independence and a member of the presidential administrations of John Adams, Jefferson, and Madison: "Such is my veneration for every religion that reveals the attributes of the Deity, or a future state of rewards and punishments, that I had rather see the opinions of Confucius or Mahomed inculcated upon our youth than see them grow up wholly devoid of a system of religious principles. But the religion I mean to recommend in this place is that of the New Testament."[5]

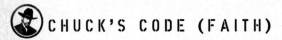 CHUCK'S CODE (FAITH)

I will maintain an attitude of open-mindedness toward another person's viewpoint, while still holding fast to that which I know to be true and honest. (#9 of my Principles for Life)

#80

OFFICIAL CHUCK
NORRIS FACT

"According to Einstein's theory of relativity, Chuck Norris can actually roundhouse kick you yesterday."

LET'S BE HONEST . . .

Speaking of kicking and yesterday, my very first speaking role in a movie was 1968 in *The Wrecking Crew*, starring Dean Martin and Elke Sommer. Bruce Lee actually got me the part. He was the fight coordinator and wanted me to do a fight scene with Dean.

☆ **222** ☆

In the scene, I'm sitting on a stool at the bar in a nightclub. Dean enters, and as he walks past me, I step in front of him, stick out my hand, and say, "May I, Mr. Helm?" implying that I want his gun. Later in the scene, Dean and I get into a big fight.

Sounds fairly simple, doesn't it? I studied my line, "May I, Mr. Helm?" for days, trying to figure out the best delivery. I said it strongly, coolly, smoothly, and so on. Then the day came to film the scene. With cameras rolling, Dean Martin entered on cue. As he came closer to me, I could feel my throat tightening up and my body getting rigid. As I stepped in front of him for my big moment, "May I, Mr. Helm?" came out in a barely audible whisper. Dean handed me his pistol and stepped past me. I sat back down, angry at myself for not being able to say one line.

Soon we began the fight scene. Dean was to be photographed in the first stage of the fight, and then his fight double would take over. For the opening shot, I was to throw a spinning heel kick over Dean's head. I asked him how far he planned to drop, so I could calculate how close I could kick over his head. He told me not to worry, and he bent his knees about halfway to the floor. I said, "That's great."

When the director called, "Action!" Dean forgot to bend his knees. I hit him flush on the shoulder, sending him flying across the room. The director was horrified, but Dean was good-natured about it and said, "I'm okay. Let's do that again." When we did the retake, I decided to kick way over Dean's head, just in case he didn't drop again, but this time he sank down to a squatting position and my kick went about four feet over his head. After that, his fight double came in, and the scene came off great.

"A celebrity is any well-known television or movie star who looks like he spends more than two hours working on his hair."

> STEVE MARTIN

CHUCK'S CODE (FIGHT)

Be humble about your accomplishments. If
not, humility will be your teacher.

"The term 'dead ringer' refers to anyone sitting near Chuck Norris in a movie theater who forgets to turn off his cell phone."

LET'S BE HONEST . . .

The Bible says to give honor to whom honor is due (see Romans 13:7). I don't speak about the integrity of famous people very often because it is a trait that is often difficult to find. But there is one person whom I have respected for many years as a man of integrity. That person is Denzel Washington.

Throughout Denzel's years as a successful actor, he has stayed grounded in his faith and committed to his family. Unfortunately, too many entertainers in Hollywood have been led astray by their popularity, money, and power—myself included. Thank the Lord I found my way back before it was too late.

I've met Denzel only once—at a boxing match, no less—and when I looked him in the eye, I saw a very gracious man with a humble heart and a warrior's spirit. I believe that is why he is one of the most popular actors in the world. Of course, having incredible talent doesn't hurt. But what impresses me about Denzel is that he has not let the temptations of Hollywood negatively affect his faith or his relationship with his family.

I was a fan of his before I met him, and I became a huge fan after meeting him—which very seldom happens when I meet a famous person. I love this quote from Denzel that I recently read: "I'm a regular guy with a great job."[1]

One thing is certain: Denzel may be "a regular guy," but he's not ordinary—in God's eyes or mine!

THEY SAID IT . . .

"I've worked in a factory. I was a garbage man. I worked in a post office. It's not that long ago. I like to think that I'm just a regular guy." > DENZEL WASHINGTON

CHUCK'S CODE (FIGHT)

"I will always be as enthusiastic about the success of others as I am about my own." (#8 of my Principles for Life)

"Chuck Norris can crush facts with his bare opinion."

LET'S BE HONEST . . .

I'm not an economist, but this much I have figured out: If our spending is always more than our income, we're heading down the wrong fiscal road. That's where we've been for quite some time as a nation. Outside brief periods in our history, we've never been very disciplined with debt management.

On January 1, 1791, during George Washington's second year as president, the national debt was $75,463,476.52.[1] On September 30, 2007, the government estimated the balance owed at $9,007,653,372,262.48. Our annual trade deficit is a staggering eight hundred billion dollars, up from thirty-eight billion dollars in 1993—including a ninety-billion-dollar deficit with Mexico and $250 billion with China. Of course, with trillions of dollars more being added to our national debt via big government bailouts, we are burying future generations in a massive monetary morass.

Our founders created this country to experience freedom from tyranny and domination. Do we think we can experience liberty, either politically or personally, when our private and national debts loom over us like the king of England once did?

Though the Revolutionary War took its toll on the financial strength of the nation (as wars always do), most ardent patriots didn't want to see the country accrue any further obligations. Shedding light on the need for fiscal responsibility was Thomas Jefferson, who had quite a bit of financial advice to offer the new nation.[2]

Here is one of his timely pearls of wisdom:

> We must make our election between economy and liberty, or profusion and servitude. If we run into such debts as that we must be taxed in our meat and in our drink, in our necessaries and our comforts, in our labors and our amusements, for our callings and our creeds, as the people of England are, our people, like them, must come to labor sixteen hours in the twenty-four, give the earnings of fifteen of these to the government for their debts and daily expenses, and the

sixteenth being insufficient to afford us bread, we must live, as they now do, on oatmeal and potatoes, have no time to think, no means of calling the mismanagers to account, but be glad to obtain subsistence by hiring ourselves to rivet their chains on the necks of our fellow-sufferers.[3]

THEY SAID IT . . .
"The maxim of buying nothing without the money in our pockets to pay for it would make of our country one of the happiest on earth." > THOMAS JEFFERSON[4]

(★) CHUCK'S CODE (FREEDOM)

Debt in any form is a form of repression. Nationally or personally, debt is bondage, plain and simple. When we're not in debt, we're free to live, move, and enjoy our being.

"Although it is
not common
knowledge,
there are
exactly
three sides
to the Force:
the light side,
the dark side,
and the Chuck
Norris side."

LET'S BE HONEST . . .

When I think of great forces and lights across this land, I think of
the plethora of private schools that offer exceptional education and
training for life.

I have been humbled many times in my life, but I think my
greatest humbling experience was when I was invited to give the

commencement speech for the graduating class at one of those schools—Liberty University.

When Jerry Falwell Jr., the chancellor of the university, called and asked if I would speak at their commencement, I replied, "This is a great honor, but why did you pick me?"

"I didn't," he said. "The students picked you."

Taken aback by what he said, I accepted.

The commencement ceremony was on May 10, 2008, in Lynchburg, Virginia. As I stepped up to the podium to speak to the graduating students and their families, I thought to myself, *Here I am, a guy who barely graduated from high school, growing up shy and introverted, standing up here ready to speak to all these people.* Talk about humbling!

I told the crowd of more than twenty thousand (the largest turnout in the university's history) that I have a difficult time with public speaking and that this was my first commencement speech at any university. Still, I shared my experiences growing up and how nothing is impossible in this great country of ours with God on your side. I shared with them about my struggles growing up and my drifting from God, but how He never left me. I explained that when I finally did get right with the Lord and began reading the Bible, I came upon Proverbs 16:9: "A man's heart plans his way, but the LORD directs his steps" (NKJV). I realized that even though I had drifted from my faith earlier in my life, the Lord still had plans for me. I believe that's true with all of us.

After my speech—and much to my surprise—Jerry Falwell Jr. awarded me with an honorary doctorate of humanities. As I put on the black robe and Jerry fastened the doctoral sash around my neck, I was overwhelmed and deeply honored. I have the degree hanging proudly in my living room.

"What an honor and what a surprise for a boy born in England, raised in Cleveland, and schooled in vaudeville." > BOB HOPE, ON BEING TOLD HE WAS BEING AWARDED AN HONORARY KNIGHTHOOD

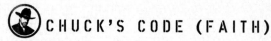

CHUCK'S CODE (FAITH)

Fame is fleeting. What counts is what you contribute.

"There is no such thing as global warming. Chuck Norris was cold, so he turned up the sun."

LET'S BE HONEST . . .

I'll never forget turning up the heat on my friends and television hosts Regis Philbin and Kathie Lee Gifford.

While filming *Walker, Texas Ranger*, and newly married to Gena, I was invited to appear on *Live with Regis and Kathie Lee*.

I let Regis know that I was going to play a joke on Kathie Lee and let him in on it. Here's how it played out.

On the morning of the show, Regis and Kathie Lee were interviewing me about my TV series. I explained that I would like to work more on my romantic side because all I had done up until then was play action heroes. I elaborated with some frustration, however, that I just didn't know how well I could do with a tender romantic scene.

I looked in Kathie Lee's direction and said to her, "Could I practice a scene for you to see what you think?" She replied, "Okay." So I looked to the audience and asked for a volunteer.

I picked a beautiful blonde woman in the crowd. I brought her over to the chair and had her sit down. I said to the woman, "Let's just say we are filming a scene where I am going to ask for your hand in marriage and you can respond however you want. Is that all right with you?"

She said, "Sure!"

"By the way," I asked, "what is your name?"

"Natalie."

"Okay, Natalie, here goes."

I then got down on my knee and took her hand. "Natalie, you are the love of my life, and I cannot imagine spending my life without you. So I am asking you from the bottom of my heart, 'Will you marry me?'"

Natalie responded with an emphatic, "Yes!" So I excitedly stood up, grabbed her, leaned her back in my arms, and planted a kiss on her that lasted almost a full minute!

Natalie's arms were waving from the passionate kiss. Kathie Lee's eyes were popping out of her head! She just couldn't believe I would pull a woman from the audience and lay that big of a kiss on her.

Finally, I stopped the lip-lock and said to Kathie Lee, "I would like you to meet my wife, Gena!"

CHUCK'S CODE (FITNESS)

Learn to laugh with people. If you don't, they'll laugh at you.

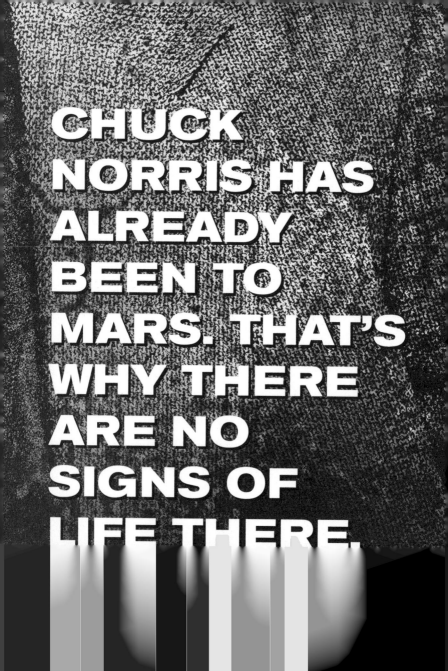

"How much wood would a woodchuck chuck if a woodchuck could Chuck Norris? All of it."

LET'S BE HONEST . . .

Years ago, during my competitive martial arts days, I was asked by my attorney friend David Glickman to testify in court as a professional witness. He explained that he was defending someone who was pleading self-defense after shooting a man who was a black belt in karate.

David planned his defense along the lines that a black-belt practitioner's karate skill is considered to be a deadly weapon and thus the defendant's claim of self-defense was valid. David said, "With your being a world champion, your testimony could be invaluable."

On the day of the trial, I was called to the witness stand to testify for the defendant, and then I was cross-examined by the assistant district attorney. The first words out of the DA's mouth were, "Do you expect the court to believe that a black belt in karate would have a chance against a man with a gun?"

I replied, "It's possible, depending on the distance."

"How about ten feet?" the DA asked.

I said, "If the gun wasn't already cocked and aimed, I believe it is possible."

Exasperated, the DA told me to step down from the witness stand. Then he ordered me to stand and wait in front of the jury. He then walked over to the bailiff and said, "Please remove the cartridges from your gun and give it to me." The DA then joined me in front of the jury with the empty gun in his hand. He made a show of pacing off ten feet and then faced me, saying, "I want you to stop me before I can cock and fire the gun."

What have I gotten myself into? I thought.

The DA held the gun at his side and instructed the bailiff to say, "Go." The bailiff shouted, "Go!" and before the DA could cock the gun, I had my foot planted on his chest. (I didn't follow through with my kick, because I didn't want to hurt him.)

The DA was mad. "Let's do it again," he said. "My thumb slipped."

So the bailiff gave the word, and again I planted my foot on the DA's chest before he could cock the gun.

David Glickman and I had dinner that evening, and he was laughing so hard he could hardly eat. He said, "I will never forget that look on the DA's face. You should have kicked him across the room."

"I don't think that would have been a good idea," I said.

"Well, anyway," David said. "The DA made a big mistake by asking a question to which he didn't know the answer."

THEY SAID IT . . .
"Whenever you're scared of something, don't let that define you. We all feel it, but step up." > VINCE VAUGHN

 CHUCK'S CODE (FIGHT)

Don't underestimate your competition.
Be optimistic; but be a realist, too.

"When Chuck Norris crosses the street, the cars look both ways."

LET'S BE HONEST . . .

We equate power with dominance, rule, and self-glorification, which is unfortunate. I believe that when God created us in his image, he gave us the authority and autonomy to rule the earth, not one another. Power was given to serve, not to enslave. As I've taught countless martial arts students over the years, the greatest form of power is *restraint* and the ability to harness that potential to help others.

Great leaders have always understood this power principle. Jesus, who modeled God's original intent for our autonomy, said, "Whoever wants to be a leader among you must be your servant, and whoever wants to be first among you must become your slave. For even the Son of Man came not to be served but to serve others and to give his life as a ransom for many."[1]

When we don't properly recognize and utilize the power that God has granted us, we naturally abuse it. An example of this can be found in my now-deceased father.

Dad was generally a good man when he was sober, but sobriety was not one of his strengths. When he was drunk, the littlest things would send him into a rage. If he heard the water running while he was suffering from a hangover, he would explode in an abusive tirade, roaring threats and expletives against everyone in the house. The devil might be in the details, but he's also in the bottle—I've seen his spirit at work.

Growing up, my most difficult and confusing relationship was with my father. He had abandoned his role as a servant-leader, model, and mentor, and he dodged his duties and authority by drinking himself into a constant stupor. As a result, he failed the highest calling of every father—to reflect a shadow of God's image to his children. He failed to see that what gives a father unique power is that he bears the same title and reflection of our heavenly Father.

Some recent studies show that fathers are finally reacting to the mother-knows-best mentality that has dominated families for the past several decades. One study in particular, published in the

Journal of Family Psychology, reveals that more husbands want to be an equal parenting partner, not just a "hired hand."[2]

Fathers were designed to show their children what God is like. In that sense, a father is a child's first Sunday school. Or, as George Herbert said, "One father is more than a hundred schoolmasters."

THEY SAID IT . . .

"Manhood and Christlikeness are synonymous." > EDWIN LOUIS COLE, PIONEER OF THE CHRISTIAN MEN'S MOVEMENT[3]

CHUCK'S CODE (FAMILY)

Reflecting the image of God to our children is our greatest power and our most important duty.

"Chuck Norris doesn't step on toes; he steps on necks."

LET'S BE HONEST . . .

The Octagon was the biggest and best martial arts film of my career. There were many fight scenes, but one in particular I remember most vividly.

We were filming inside a walled-in enclosure that was the

headquarters of the ninjas. We started filming the fights at six o'clock in the evening, and by four o'clock the next morning, everyone was exhausted (including me). The director told the fight coordinator, who was my brother Aaron, that we would finish the fight scenes the next day. So Aaron sent home the four stuntmen I was to fight. Five minutes later, the director changed his mind and decided to keep filming. Aaron protested that the stuntmen had already left, but the director told him to figure something out.

There were two other stuntmen, not in the original cast, who were still on the set, so Aaron recruited them. Their identities would be hidden by the ninja outfits and masks, so there was no problem with continuity from earlier filmed scenes. Aaron decided to play the third ninja himself, but we were still missing a fourth ninja.

Just then, one of the extras on the film, a well-built young man, stepped up and volunteered. Aaron asked him, "Have you ever done any stunt work before?"

"No," he said, "but I'm in great shape, and I believe I can do it."

Aaron said, "Chuck makes a little contact when he hits. Are you sure?"

The young man said, "That's okay with me. I'm in great shape, so don't worry about it."

Aaron gave the young man a ninja outfit and laid out the scene in which I was to walk into a maze and be attacked by the four ninjas. The newcomer was to attempt to grab me from behind. I would then back-kick him in the stomach, and he would go down. After rehearsal, I told Aaron to put a chest pad under the young man's ninja shirt so I wouldn't have to worry about hurting him. But the man refused, saying. "The others aren't wearing pads, so I don't need one either."

The cameras started rolling, and the director called, "Action." When the young man, who was first to attack, tried to grab me, I back-kicked him in the stomach. His eyes rolled back in his head, and he dropped to the ground groaning.

Oh no, I thought, *I've hurt him*. But the cameras were still rolling, and the second ninja stepped up to attack me. I quickly turned to him, but I had forgotten what I was supposed to do for the scene. So I shifted sideways and punched him in the side of the head, knocking him out. Aaron, the third ninja, heard the contact but jumped out at me anyway. I spun instinctively and roundhouse-kicked him in the head, knocking him out too. The fourth ninja was on top of a building and was supposed to jump down on top of me, but he looked down at the inert bodies and shouted, "I'm not coming down there!" Fortunately, everyone recovered, and we reshot the scene the next day with the original stuntmen. What a night!

THEY SAID IT . . .
"A lot of people ask me when I do a stunt, 'Jackie, are you scared?' Of course I'm scared. I'm not Superman." > JACKIE CHAN

CHUCK'S CODE (FIGHT)

Pain is temporary. Film is forever. So let's go for it!

"When Bruce Banner gets mad, he turns into the Hulk. When the Hulk gets mad, he turns into Chuck Norris."

LET'S BE HONEST . . .

Irritability is often caused by not eating well or not getting enough sleep or rest. It happens to me, and I bet it happens to you. If we don't sleep, we get grumpy. If we eat lots of sugar, we experience mood swings. We are what we consume, and we need to remember that we can direct much of what we feel and detour many of the bad feelings. Health care is largely about preventative care, not prescriptive care. We need to get off the track of being consumed with treating our problems and get onto the track of preventing them.

I believe the answer to the present health-care crisis in America begins with the American public and not with governmental intervention or bureaucracy that would mandate socialized medicine. Our Founding Fathers never could have imagined a government that would micromanage civilian diets by creating a Food and Drug Administration or Department of Agriculture. Thomas Jefferson quipped, "W[ere] the government to prescribe to us our medicine and diet, our bodies would be in such keeping as our souls are now."[1] Our founders' health-care system was a very simple one: Take care of your health.

We don't need to pay billions of dollars through new taxes to provide universal medical coverage. If anything, I believe the government needs to discover more ways to motivate personal responsibility and disease prevention, encourage the states' role as stages for new market-based ideas, and challenge the private sector to seek creative ways to bring down medical costs. Most of all, if we took better care of ourselves, we could reduce our personal and national medical costs and live longer and happier at the same time.

The Bible calls our bodies temples of God's spirit.[2] If we want to live at our optimum, we need to return to treating our bodies like temples instead of like trash bins. As Dr. Don Colbert says, "Eating bad is not going to keep us out of heaven, but it will get us there a lot quicker!"[3]

"French fries. I love them. Some people are chocolate and sweets people. I love French fries. That and caviar." > CAMERON DIAZ

CHUCK'S CODE (FITNESS)

Don't forget the push-ups, or you might be pushing up daisies sooner than you'd like.

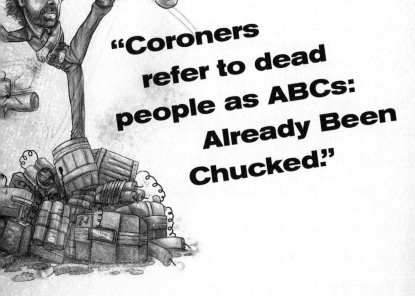

"Coroners refer to dead people as ABCs: Already Been Chucked."

LET'S BE HONEST . . .

If it were up to my early critics, I would have been "chucked" a long time ago.

When I starred in my first truly successful film, *Good Guys Wear Black*, the critics crucified me. They said I was the worst actor they had ever seen since the silent-film era. My feelings were really hurt, and I told Steve McQueen about it.

Steve said to me, "Don't worry about what the critics think. What really matters is what the audience thinks. If they come to see your movies, it doesn't matter what the critics say." Steve was absolutely correct, and for more than thirty years I've been living by that advice.

President Teddy Roosevelt put it this way:

> It is not the critic who counts; not the man who points out how the strong man stumbles, or where the doer of deeds could have done them better. The credit belongs to the man who is actually in the arena, whose face is marred by dust and sweat and blood; who strives valiantly; who errs, and comes short again and again, because there is no effort without error and shortcoming; but who does actually strive to do the deeds; who knows the great enthusiasms, the great devotions; who spends himself in a worthy cause; who at the best knows in the end the triumph of high achievement and who, at the worst, if he fails, at least he fails while daring greatly, so that his place shall never be with those cold and timid souls who knew neither victory nor defeat.[1]

Those are words we all can live by.

There's another nugget of wisdom that Steve McQueen passed along to me when I was a new actor that really inspired and shaped my characters for the rest of my film and television career. He said, "I suggest you cut down on all your dialogue. Let your costars do all the trivial dialogue, and when there is something important to say, then you be the one to say it."

He explained, "I did that in my film *Bullitt*. I had a scene with Robert Vaughn where I had to reply to him. My dialogue was three paragraphs long. I scratched it all out and instead said, 'You work your side of the street and I'll work mine.' People still remember that line.

"Remember," Steve told me, "sometimes less is more." I have never forgotten that.

THEY SAID IT . . .
"We are not trying to entertain the critics. I'll take my chances with the public." > WALT DISNEY

CHUCK'S CODE (FITNESS)

I will give so much time to the improvement of myself that I will have no time to criticize others. (#7 of my Principles for Life)

#90

"Chuck Norris never loses his way, because all roads lead to Chuck Norris."

LET'S BE HONEST . . .

Webster defines *lose* as "to cause to miss one's way or bearings; to make (oneself) withdrawn from immediate reality; to wander or go astray from; to draw away from." Being lost comes from having no boundaries, no directions, no map, and no guidelines. It's as true nationally as it is individually.

Individually, we seek meaning, purpose, and peace in a passionately hedonistic culture, only to come up repeatedly empty handed and unfulfilled. We believe that power, pleasure, position, possessions, or places will fill the longing within our hearts, only to obtain these things and then discover an inner vacuum that has grown to twice the size and needs double the amount to be satisfied. No one is immune to these vicious, visceral cycles, including me.

We all lose our way from time to time—and when we do, we must be willing to admit it. But many people respond like Daniel Boone, who once said, "I have never been lost, but I will admit to being confused for several weeks." That's funny, but we all know there is no way we can find our way home until we first confess to having lost our way.

I understand what it means to be lost—what it means to never feel satisfied. In my autobiography, *Against All Odds*, I admit that I succumbed to the enticements of fame and fortune, like so many before me. I swallowed the Hollywood lifestyle, hook, line, and sinker. I had notoriety and riches at my fingertips, but I never felt like it was quite enough. Fulfillment seemed always just beyond my grasp.

I thought I had everything—money, fame, and so on—but all I really had was a huge hole in my heart.

I finally understood what the Founding Fathers told us two hundred years ago, my mom told me more than sixty years ago, and my wife told me twelve years ago: "Without God, we will have empty lives."

It was then that I found my way home. Jesus said, "[I] came to seek and save those who are lost."[1] I was lost, but now I'm found.

"I once was lost but now am found—
Was blind, but now I see."

> JOHN NEWTON, "AMAZING GRACE"

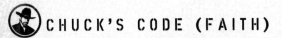 **CHUCK'S CODE (FAITH)**

Never be too proud to ask for directions—even life directions.

"Lightning never strikes twice in the same place, because Chuck Norris is looking for it."

LET'S BE HONEST . . .

In our **KICKSTART KIDS** program, we teach middle school students how martial arts training relates to daily life. If we think of the studio as a microcosm of the world in which we live, then we can see that proper training can help us discover our weaknesses and strengths. Our lives are composed of a series of engagements and problems to be solved.

The solutions learned in the studio can often be applied to real life. For instance, martial arts training teaches self-control. If your tendency is to respond to a physical or verbal altercation with aggression or harsh words, then you will create an enemy. But if you react with a soft response, you may be able to control the situation in a peaceful manner—and possibly make a friend. This is what we teach in the martial arts classroom.

As a martial arts fighter, I realized I had to possess the inner strength in staring down the impossible, to face giant opponents, often alone, in order to become six-time world middleweight karate champion. Many times I fought opponents who were stronger and faster than me. I knew that, in order to win, I must study the weaknesses of my opponents, visualize my victory, and persevere to win. But in real life, learning to back down can be your biggest ally. Avoiding altercations can be your greatest strength. Power doesn't have to be proven.

The Bible says in Proverbs 15:1 that a gentle answer turns away wrath. I truly believe that. Insults, even threats, are not worthy of physical or verbal combat. Like I said, it is always better to try to make a friend than an enemy.

Martial arts training teaches you to remain calm at all times, to consider alternatives, and to try your very best to avoid meeting force with force. A person who is physically and mentally prepared seems to very seldom encounter altercations.

Prepare yourself on the mat, and you can avoid a situation on the street.

THEY SAID IT . . .

"The best way to destroy an enemy is to make him a friend."

> ABRAHAM LINCOLN

 CHUCK'S CODE (FIGHT)

It's just as easy to make a friend as it is to make an enemy. If you're hostile, expect a hostile response from others. Whatever you project is what you will usually receive in return.

OFFICIAL CHUCK NORRIS FACT #92

"Chuck Norris is the reason Waldo is hiding."

LET'S BE HONEST . . .

The question probably asked most of me about my friend Bruce Lee is, Do you think you could have beaten Bruce Lee in a professional competition?

The truth is Bruce was a formidable opponent with a chiseled physique and excellent technique. I always enjoyed working out and spending time with him. He was as charismatic in person as he was on film. His confidence and wit were dazzling, and sometimes even debilitating to others.

One time, when we both lived in Southern California, I was over at Bruce's house. In his garage, he had several mannequins set up for practicing martial art techniques. He was particularly proud of one with a head that bobbled.

"Do a kick to its head," he said with a smile.

I was wearing some pretty tight denim jeans (remember the 1970s?), so I told him, "Not with these pants." After a little more prodding by Bruce, I snapped my leg up, roundhouse-kicking the dummy in the head and jostling it like a teeter-totter in fast motion. But my jeans tore in two at the crotch and literally dropped down to my ankles! Bruce got a big laugh out of that one!

Bruce was lightning fast, very agile, and incredibly strong for his size, but he never competed professionally. If he had, I believe he would have been a world champion.[1]

Bruce Lee learned from everybody. He had a very open mind. He never believed that only one martial arts style was superior. He believed that everything had strengths and weaknesses and that we should find the strengths in each method.

When I first started working out with Bruce, he only believed in kicking below the waist, from his training in Wing Chun. I encouraged him not to limit himself and to at least develop the ability to kick high, whether he used it or not. I started doing my spinning heel kicks and hitting the pads. Then Bruce started doing it. Within six months, he could kick as well as anyone.

Okay, enough stalling! So would I have beaten Bruce Lee in a real competition or not? Well, the fact is that Bruce was my friend, not my opponent. And besides, if you'll forgive me for answering with another one of Bruce's classic lines: "Showing off is the fool's idea of glory."

THEY SAID IT . . .

"What you feed your mind is just as important as what you feed your body, because what you feed on is what you become."

> GENA NORRIS, WIFE OF THE "FACT MAN"

 CHUCK'S CODE (FIGHT)

Cherish the friendships you make in this life.
Protect them as you would your own life.

OFFICIAL CHUCK NORRIS FACT

"Chuck Norris uses Tabasco sauce for eye drops."

LET'S BE HONEST . . .

During my years in the acting field, I have had the opportunity to travel all over the world. The trip I most enjoyed was a safari vacation with my wife, Gena. We took along two friends who are black belts, Bob Green and Howard Jackson, for security.

We started in Johannesburg, South Africa, visiting Victoria Falls and canoeing up the Zambezi River. Then we traveled to Botswana, where we began our safari. At night, we could hear elephants—and no telling what else—milling around outside as we fell asleep in our tents. The guide told us that once we were zipped into our tents for the night, we had to stay put.

I don't have time to share with you all the other great stories of the trip, but one I just have to tell is about the night safari we took. There were seven of us, including a driver, our guide, and the game spotter, who had a spotlight mounted on the hood of the open jeep. Gena and I were in the middle, and Howard and Bob were in the back.

As we drove around in the bush, the spotter shone his light on various nocturnal animals, and our guide explained something about each one. As we went around a particular bend in the road, the spotlight illumined a mother elephant and her baby calf. The mother got startled by the light and let out a huge bellow with her trunk as she shoved her baby off to the side with her body. We quickly drove on by.

Bob suddenly said that he heard something behind us. I turned around, but it was so dark I couldn't even see my hand in front of my face. A few moments later, Howard said, "I hear something behind us too!" The spotter turned his light toward the rear of the vehicle, and sure enough, the mother elephant was charging us! When the light hit her again, she let out another roaring bellow with her trunk and lowered her head to ram us with her long tusks.

Our hearts were pounding, and the adrenaline was flowing. We started screaming, "Drive faster, drive faster, she's right on our tail!" The driver put the pedal to the metal, and we somehow managed to outrun the angry elephant. After that experience, we headed straight back to camp, having had enough excitement for the night.

THEY SAID IT . . .

"Another thing that has helped to build security in our relationship is that we pray together about anything in our family or ministry that looks challenging. There's a great sense of peace and oneness that comes from going to God together and placing a difficult matter in His hands." > DR. GARY SMALLEY (www.garysmalley.com)[1]

CHUCK'S CODE (FAMILY)

Don't ever stop being friends and having fun in marriage—the two ingredients absent from every failing marriage and present in every successful one.

"Chuck Norris counted to infinity— twice."

LET'S BE HONEST . . .

Counting cash or commodities is generally how most people calculate their worth. I used to think the American dream could be obtained through the accumulation of possessions, positions, and prestige.

Have you ever noticed in the Declaration of Independence that life and liberty are coupled with *happiness*, not with wealth, status, or materialism? Why not the latter? Because they are fleeting and fluctuating, just like the stock market.

Our founders didn't put their dreams or security in material abundance. George Washington had to borrow money to get to his own inauguration. Thomas Jefferson died one hundred thousand dollars in debt. Some dream of material prosperity! Most of the Founding Fathers lived modestly and were willing to share what they had—and even contribute to government—to build up other Americans.

The one constant in life, the one thing on which our founders based their security, is our *Creator*. He is so important that our founders mentioned him in the Declaration of Independence as the source of all things. They trusted not in the supply but in the Supplier to acquire life, liberty, and happiness, and they encouraged us to do the same.

There's a verse in the Bible that summarizes this idea for me: "Teach those who are rich in this world not to be proud and not to trust in their money, which is so unreliable. Their trust should be in God, who richly gives us all we need for our enjoyment."[1]

God is our national treasure, buried in the sands of history and believed in universally by all of America's Founding Fathers. And He can be our treasure, too, if only we would rediscover that He is still at the heart of the Founding Fathers' dream for this country. He can help us align our priorities with His and bring us true fulfillment in this life. God is the key.

I have been asked what time in my life I would like to go back to. I tell people that there is no time in my life that fills me with more joy than my life right now. Why is that? Because I have an incredible relationship with my wife, my seven children, and my eleven grandchildren. And my mom, who is eighty-eight years old and going strong, is the matriarch of the whole clan. Honestly, I never had true peace in my life until Gena and I moved to our ranch in Texas and started evaluating what was truly important in our lives. It boils down to this: God, marriage, family, friends, and our foundation, **KICKSTART KIDS**.

When you've got God, you've got the gold—and everything you need to achieve and experience the American dream.

THEY SAID IT . . .
"When you understand that your self-worth is not determined by your net worth, then you'll have financial freedom." > SUZE ORMAN

CHUCK'S CODE (FREEDOM)

The freedom our founders enjoyed is discovered
independent of our stuff or our savings.

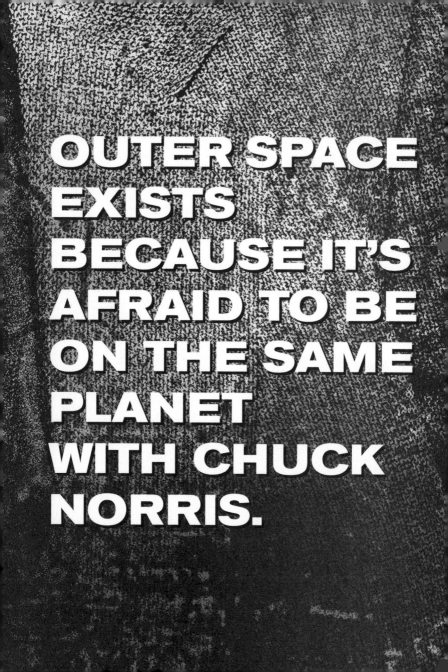

"Chuck Norris is so fast that he can run around the world and punch himself in the back of the head."

LET'S BE HONEST . . .

After one of her private karate lessons with me, Priscilla Presley invited me to Las Vegas to watch Elvis perform at the Hilton Hotel. I gladly accepted the invitation. This was the first time I met Elvis in person. I'll never forget sitting in the front booth with Priscilla at that dinner show and being captivated by Elvis's charisma and showmanship.

Afterward, Elvis invited us up to his suite, where we talked until four o'clock in the morning. At first I thought, *What are we going to talk about?* I knew nothing about music, but I knew I could talk about martial arts all night long. And we did. I was impressed with Elvis's insight into and devotion to the martial arts. Even after two shows that evening, he stayed up till the early morning hours shooting the breeze with us.

Like me, Elvis was introduced to the world of self-defense when he was in the military. Throughout his life, he studied many styles under several different instructors. In 1958, he started as a student under the German master Juergen Seydel (a Shotokan sensei), then he was mentored under Tetsugio Murakami (a Japanese Shotokan master), Kang Rhee (a Korean Sa-Ryu Tae Kwon Do grandmaster), Americans Ed Parker (the founder of American Kenpo and Elvis's lifelong teacher) and Henry Slomanski (under whom Elvis earned his black belt), and Filipino Dan Inosanto (later a student of Bruce Lee).

Over the next decade and a half, Elvis was awarded advancing black belt degrees, and in time he was granted an honorary seventh degree black belt. He even opened his own martial arts school in Memphis, the Tennessee Karate Institute, where Bill Wallace was the chief instructor.

Elvis was a really nice, down-to-earth guy who made you feel in a few hours like you had known him forever. I still enjoy his music.

THEY SAID IT . . .
"If life were fair, Elvis would be alive and all the impersonators would be dead." > JOHNNY CARSON

CHUCK'S CODE (FIGHT)

Don't be an impersonator; be a trendsetter. Don't just be a follower; be a leader. Go against the tide, because, as you know, the only thing that goes with the tide is a dead fish.

"Chuck Norris's favorite cut of meat is a roundhouse."

LET'S BE HONEST . . .

I'm from Texas, and I love a good steak. I try to take good care of my body by balancing my diet with regular exercise, but I'm equally concerned for my total health—my total being.

You are more than a physical being; you are a holistic creature. Your body is more than a shell. It houses an eternal spirit, and how you nourish it affects your mind, body, and soul. They are all interrelated. Each affects the other in some way. And we need to nourish each in a balanced way. Thomas Jefferson spoke to this connection when he said, "Health must not be sacrificed to learning. A strong body makes the mind strong."[1]

Thousands of health care professionals—including physicians at the National Cancer Institute, the Mayo Clinic, and the National Center for Complementary and Alternative Medicine—concur about the power that one's religious practice has on his or her total well-being.[2] A recent study shows that 54 percent of Americans have heard from someone they know that the Bible helped and encouraged them during the past six months.[3]

That is why thousands of years ago, the Scriptures proclaimed, "Trust in the LORD with all your heart; . . . Then you will have healing for your body and strength for your bones."[4] Even Jesus Himself said, "People do not live by bread alone, but by every word that comes from the mouth of God."[5]

When I first met Gena, I had drifted from God and was living the secular life of a celebrity. I had fame and fortune, but I also had a huge hole in my heart. Gena brought me back to my faith by morning Bible reading. At first, she did all the reading, but as soon as the Holy Spirit grabbed me and filled the hole in my heart, I took over the reading. To this day, as soon as we get up, we start the day reading a chapter from the Bible. It helps us to start the day on the right foot.

If you'd like to begin a spiritual exercise, I recommend that you read a chapter a day from the book of Proverbs in the Bible— there is one for every day of the month. I like to read from the New International Version (I have a *Life Application Study Bible*), for its simple readability. I also recommend a daily serving of the *Our Daily Bread* devotional, which is now available online and is a great source of inspiration for successful living.[6]

"First you forget names; then you forget faces. Next, you forget to pull your zipper up; and finally you forget to pull it down."

> COMEDIAN GEORGE BURNS

CHUCK'S CODE (FITNESS)

We are mind, body, and spirit, so take care of your total self.

"Chuck Norris's first job was as a paperboy. There were no survivors."

LET'S BE HONEST . . .

The first time *Walker, Texas Ranger* became a top-ten show (a real accomplishment for a show airing on Saturday night), it was for a faith-based episode called "The Neighborhood."

The episode is about a twelve-year-old African-American girl who lives in the ghetto outside of Dallas. While walking home from school one day, she gets caught in the middle of a gang war and is accidentally shot and critically wounded.

She is in the hospital when Walker arrives to investigate the incident. Walker is informed by her doctor that she is bleeding internally and that nothing can be done to save her. The little girl is dying.

Then, miraculously, she recovers, leaving the doctor in total shock. She explains that she was on her way to heaven when an angel stopped her and told her that it was not her time—that she still had a job to do on earth and that was to clean up her neighborhood.

At the end of the episode, she motivates the people in the neighborhood to clean up the graffiti and chase the drug dealers out. At a Christian revival meeting, she convinces the two rival gangs to come together peacefully.

I loved that episode, and the message was clear: If we would all work together as God intended, the world would definitely change for the better. I believe that with all my heart.

A new seven-year study of the top 275 movies, published in Ted Baehr's *Movieguide*, yielded the information that Americans really do prefer more conservative, pro-American movies with traditional, Judeo-Christian values and free market ideals rather than movies pushing an anti-capitalist, socialist, atheist, Communist, or anti-Christian agenda.[1] They discovered that conservative movies on average earned more than three times the box office revenues of liberal movies.

It's no wonder "The Neighborhood" was a top-ten *Walker, Texas Ranger* episode.

CHUCK'S CODE (FIGHT)

Education is to the mind as God's Word is to the heart.

CHUCK NORRIS BRINGS THE NOISE

AND THE FUNK

"Chuck Norris was banned from competitive bull riding after he rode his bucking bull from Austin to Oklahoma City to pick up his dry cleaning."

LET'S BE HONEST . . .

Most people know me from my martial arts, movie, and television careers. But not many know that I've also competed outside those arenas.

During breaks between my filming schedules, I would get

antsy, so when I heard about celebrity off-road truck races in Las Vegas, I decided to enter one. I ended up competing in races such as the Frontier 100 off-road race, the Mint 400, and several others. My stunt-driving experience in my films and my commitment to excellence helped me to do well in these races—to the point that the sponsor of the Mint 400 decided to bring in a ringer to race against me.

The night of the pre-race party, a man walked in wearing a racing helmet that covered his face. I stared at him, trying to figure out who he might be. Then he walked up to me and took off his helmet. To my surprise, it was my brother Aaron.

Aaron is as competitive as I am and had been a stunt driver in many films, so I knew I was in for a real challenge. The following morning, when the race began, Aaron immediately took the lead. I followed close behind in second place. Throughout the race, at designated stops, I was given updates that I was closing in on Aaron's lead. He ultimately beat me by six seconds. (One more proof that sibling rivalry can be fun, too!)

Dirt racing proved to be too dusty, so I decided to switch to aquatic racing instead. I went on to set a new world record by racing a forty-six-foot V-hull Scarab boat 612 miles from the harbor in Chicago to the Renaissance Center in Detroit. I covered the distance in twelve hours, eight minutes, and forty-two seconds—beating the world record by twenty-six minutes.

I was then offered a chance to race for the owner of Popeye's Chicken in his Popeye Super Powerboat. This was a fifty-foot catamaran with jet engines capable of speeds up to 140 mph. In my second year of racing, my team and I won the World Offshore Powerboat Championship. Talk about an adrenaline rush!

"The first step toward creating an improved future is developing the ability to envision it. Vision will ignite the fire of passion that fuels our commitment to do whatever it takes to achieve excellence. Only vision allows us to transform dreams of greatness into the reality of achievement through human action. Vision has no boundaries and knows no limits. Our vision is what we become in life." > TONY DUNGY, FORMER HEAD COACH OF THE SUPER BOWL CHAMPION INDIANAPOLIS COLTS

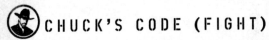 **CHUCK'S CODE (FIGHT)**

Want to improve at whatever you do? One word: Compete.

#99

OFFICIAL CHUCK NORRIS FACT

"Chuck Norris doesn't read books. He stares them down until he gets the information he wants."

LET'S BE HONEST . . .

There's something the U.S. government doesn't want you to know, and it has come out again in a new Heritage Foundation report on education: The American public is increasingly dissatisfied with public schools, and a rising number of families are opting for private education.[1] What's amazing is that, even though forty-four states have recently introduced school-choice legislation, the federal government continues to reduce options and opportunities to encourage and aid parents who want to provide their children with a private education.[2]

Of course, the government won't admit to such a blatant disregard of our rights and our interests; they insist their educational reform is seeking the good of our children. They say it is necessary to establish common educational standards. They say we need to leave education to the experts and not to parents. I fear that too many of us will simply give in to the whims of the nanny state.

I wrote about this in my *New York Times* best-selling book *Black Belt Patriotism: How to Reawaken America*:

> The reason [the government is] cracking down on private instruction has more to do with suppressing alternative education than assuring educational standards. The rationale is quite simple, though rarely if ever stated: control future generations and you control the future. So rather than letting parents be the primary educators of their children—either directly or by educating their children in the private schools of their choice—[the government wants] to deny parental rights, establish an educational monopoly run by the state, and limit private education options. It is so simple [that] any socialist can understand it. As Joseph Stalin once stated, "Education is a weapon whose effects depend on who holds it in his hands and at whom it is aimed."[3]

Is it merely coincidental that the private choice of homeschooling was outlawed by the Soviet State in 1919, by Hitler and Nazi

Germany in 1938, and by Communist China in 1949? Could our country be next?

Americans deserve educational choices. It's what our country was founded upon.

THEY SAID IT . . .

"Education is the key. But it's the kind of education . . . we teach that is the key." > EDWARD JAMES OLMOS[4]

CHUCK'S CODE (FREEDOM)

Don't check your brain at the door. Be educated, not indoctrinated.

"Chuck Norris went skydiving once but promised never to do it again. One Grand Canyon is enough."

LET'S BE HONEST . . .

In 2004, I was asked by President George H. W. Bush to skydive with him in celebration of his eightieth birthday. Yes, his eightieth! We landed in a large field near the George H. W. Bush Presidential Library in College Station, Texas.

It was an honor to jump with President Bush on that crisp, clear Lone Star day, spend some time reflecting back on the contributions of our friendship (such as how he helped me start my **KICKSTART KIDS** martial arts program for youth), and then jump in tandem with members of the U.S. Army Parachute Team, the Golden Knights.

Five years later, I was honored to receive the McLane Leadership in Business Award from President George H. W. Bush, given for my achievements in sports, entertainment, and philanthropy. I couldn't be more grateful to be chosen for that award by a man whom I have admired for more than twenty years.

On our way home after the awards evening had concluded, I asked Gena how my speech had gone. She said, "It was great, and it was so cute, too, because after you would say something funny, Drayton McLane (owner of the Houston Astros) would lean over to me and say, 'Boy, he sure is funny!' And then when you would say something endearing, President Bush would lean over to me from the other side and say, 'Boy, he sure is sweet!'"

"Oh," I said. "In other words, I'm a sweet comedian!"

In all sincerity, Gena and I feel very privileged and blessed to call President George H. W. Bush and Barbara Bush our friends. They are two of the most genuine, benevolent, and amazing people we've ever met.

"And who knows? Somewhere out in this audience may even be someone who will one day follow in my footsteps and preside over the White House as the president's spouse. I wish him well!"

> BARBARA BUSH

CHUCK'S CODE (FITNESS)

Befriend good and decent people in this life, learn from them, and model their behavior.

#101

OFFICIAL CHUCK
NORRIS FACT

"Chuck Norris's tears can cure cancer. It's too bad he's never cried."

LET'S BE HONEST . . .

If my tears could cure cancer, I would cry a million of them. Of course, that is only wishful thinking. But I do know of a substance that can cure the soul.

Mom raised my brothers and me in the Christian faith. We

didn't just attend church and Sunday school (which she taught, by the way); she also read to us from the Bible, prayed with us, and modeled a life of love. Nothing was forced down our throats—it was just lived out in front of us every day. I am who I am today because of my mom's influence.

I was twelve years old when I accepted Christ as my personal Lord and Savior and was baptized at Calvary Baptist Church, where our family attended. As a young man, I recommitted my life to Christ at a Billy Graham crusade in Los Angeles.

I've always maintained my faith throughout my martial arts, movie, and television careers, but as I shared earlier in the book, there was also a time when I lost my way. As resilient as I thought I was, I swallowed the hook of the Hollywood lifestyle.

Mom continued to pray for me throughout those years, and I'm convinced that's how and why God brought Gena into my life. She is a beacon of God's light and love, just as my mom is. Gena brought me back to my childhood faith—in which compromise was unbecoming, transparency was a virtue, humility was required, and belief was daily practiced.

On Easter Sunday 2009, I experienced another highlight in my spiritual life. I recommitted my life to Christ yet again, but this time with my household. Gena, our eight-year-old twins, and I all recommitted our lives to Christ and were baptized together by our chaplain. What an absolute joy it was to watch my loved ones go into those sacred waters and to hear them affirm their belief and recommitment to follow Jesus.

Watching them, I thought about the place in the Bible where Paul and Silas were miraculously freed from a jail cell. The jailer was so moved by the event that he asked them, "What must I do to be saved?" They replied, "Believe in the Lord Jesus, and you will be saved—you and your household." Then the jailer and all his family were baptized.[1]

As the chaplain leaned me back and fully immersed me in the water, I thought about all I had been through in my life and all I still wanted my life to be. I felt renewed, refreshed, and cleansed with the waters that are a symbol of Christ's forgiving blood. As I came up with water flowing off my head and body, I prayed as my mom has prayed every day of her life: "For your glory, Lord. For your glory!"

THEY SAID IT . . .

"Hope is the light at the end of life's tunnel. It not only makes the tunnel endurable, it fills the heart with anticipation of the world into which we will one day emerge. Not just a better world, but a new and perfect world. A world alive, fresh, beautiful, devoid of pain and suffering and war, a world without disease, without accident, without tragedy. A world without dictators and madmen. A world ruled by the only one worthy of ruling." > RANDY ALCORN (www.epm.org)[2]

CHUCK'S CODE (FAITH)

Look at life from an eternal perspective.
It will bring balance to all you do.

OFFICIAL CHUCK NORRIS FACT #10

1. "The ultimate Chuck Norris joke?" *WorldNetDaily*, October 25, 2007, http://www.wnd.com/news/article.asp?ARTICLE_ID=58339.
2. Ibid.
3. Mike Snider, "Study: Video-game-playing kids showing addiction symptoms," *USA Today*, April 21, 2009, http://www.usatoday.com/life/lifestyle/2009-04-20-gaming-addiction_N.htm.

OFFICIAL CHUCK NORRIS FACT #11

1. I encourage inquiring minds seeking proofs for the existence of God to visit the Web site and read the works of astrophysicist Dr. Hugh Ross at http://www.reasons.org/.
2. See Chuck Norris Fact #35.
3. "Science, God, and Man," *Time*, December 28, 1992.
4. Romans 1:20, isv

OFFICIAL CHUCK NORRIS FACT #13

1. See www.rachelschallenge.com.

OFFICIAL CHUCK NORRIS FACT #17

1. See http://www.daveroever.org.

OFFICIAL CHUCK NORRIS FACT #22

1. "Home Is Where the Heart Is," by Rickey Medlocke, Johnny Van Zant, Hugh Edward Thomasson Jr., and Gary Rossington, *Twenty*, Lynyrd Skynyrd, 1997.

OFFICIAL CHUCK NORRIS FACT #25

1. Clem Chambers, "New Media Revolution Winners and Losers," *Forbes*, April 5, 2007, http://www.forbes.com/home/guruinsights/2007/04/05/google-ebay-viacom-pf-guru-in_cc_0405soapbox_inl.html.

2. "Chat rooms help FBI hunt for pedophiles," *MSNBC*, May 15, 2006, http://www.msnbc.msn.com/id/12796965/.

OFFICIAL CHUCK NORRIS FACT #26

1. 1 Timothy 6:17, NASB

OFFICIAL CHUCK NORRIS FACT #28

1. "Boston thieves pull off historic robbery," *History.com*, http://www.history.com/this-day-in-history.do?action=VideoArticle&id=52345.

OFFICIAL CHUCK NORRIS FACT #34

1. "Teach Your Kids about Money," *daveramsey.com*, http://www.daveramsey.com/etc/cms/kids_teens_money_5195.htmlc.

2. For more information about Randy Alcorn's ministry, please visit www.epm.org.

3. NLT

OFFICIAL CHUCK NORRIS FACT #35

1. For a list of creation scientists, go to http://www.answersingenesis.org/home/area/bios/.

2. For a sample of Dr. Johnson's work, go to http://www.origins.org/pjohnson/pjohnson.html.

3. Dr. Colin Patterson, in a letter to Luther Sunderland, April 10, 1979. Cited in Luther D. Sunderland, *Darwin's Enigma: Fossils and Other Problems* (El Cajon, CA: Master Books, 1988), 89.

OFFICIAL CHUCK NORRIS FACT #36

1. University of Washington. "How to keep up with those New Year's resolutions, researchers find commitment is the secret of success,"

December 23, 1997, http://www.washington.edu/newsroom/news/1997archive/12-97archive/k122397.html.

OFFICIAL CHUCK NORRIS FACT #37

1. "The Chuck Norris Tribute Revolver," *AmericaRemembers.com*, http://www.americaremembers.com/products/CNTRE/CNTRE.asp.

OFFICIAL CHUCK NORRIS FACT #38

1. Expressing the sense of Congress that the President should not initiate military action against Iran without first obtaining authorization from Congress, H. Con. Res. 33, 110th Cong., 1st sess., http://www.thomas.gov/cgi-bin/query/z?c110:H.CON.RES.33.IH:.

OFFICIAL CHUCK NORRIS FACT #39

1. Psalm 68:5-6, NASB

OFFICIAL CHUCK NORRIS FACT #40

1. "Signers of the Declaration: Biographical Sketches, *National Park Service*, http://www.nps.gov/history/history/online_books/declaration/bio.htm; and "The Price They Paid," *Snopes.com*, http://www.snopes.com/history/american/pricepaid.asp.
2. The text of the Declaration of Independence can be viewed online at http://www.archives.gov/exhibits/charters/declaration_transcript.html.

OFFICIAL CHUCK NORRIS FACT #43

1. 1 Corinthians 15:58, NIV
2. Flip Baney, "Rob Bell on Sex, God, and Sex Gods," *The Wittenburg Door*, November 14, 2007, http://www.wittenburgdoor.com/interview/rob-bell.

OFFICIAL CHUCK NORRIS FACT #44

1. See Genesis 1:26-28.
2. Thomas Jefferson to Maryland Republicans, 1809.

OFFICIAL CHUCK NORRIS FACT #46

1. "Valley Forge: History and Culture," *National Park Service*, http://www.nps.gov/vafo/historyculture/index.htm.

OFFICIAL CHUCK NORRIS FACT #47

1. "Fitness," *ChuckNorris.com*, http://www.chucknorris.com/html/fitness.html.

OFFICIAL CHUCK NORRIS FACT #49

1. "Chuck Norris: An Outlaw's Worst Nightmare?" http://www.youtube.com/watch?v=GQ-lQMUn0xw.
2. Andrew Cohen, "High Noon for the Second Amendment?" *CBS News*, March 17, 2008, http://www.cbsnews.com/stories/2008/03/17/opinion/courtwatch/main3944104.shtml.
3. Professor Eugene Volokh, "Sources on the Second Amendment and Rights to Keep and Bear Arms in State Constitutions," http://www.law.ucla.edu/volokh/2amteach/sources.htm#TOC1.
4. David G. Savage, "High court takes up 2nd Amendment," *San Francisco Chronicle*, Mark 19, 2008, http://www.sfgate.com/cgi-bin/article.cgi?f=/c/a/2008/03/19/MNOOVM1PS.DTL; James Madison, the author of the Bill of Rights, wrote, "Besides the advantage of being armed, which the Americans possess over the people of almost every other nation. . . . Notwithstanding the military establishments in the several kingdoms of Europe, which are carried as far as the public resources will bear, the governments are afraid to trust the people with arms" (Federalist Paper No. 46).
5. Thomas Jefferson, letter to William Johnson, June 12, 1823, quoted in *The Complete Jefferson* (New York: Duell, Sloan & Pearce, 1943), 322.
6. Thomas Jefferson, letter to Peter Carr, August 19, 1785, http://avalon.law.yale.edu/18th_century/let31.asp.

OFFICIAL CHUCK NORRIS FACT #51

1. Chuck Norris, "Questions I Am Asked Most about Martial Arts, *WorldNetDaily*, July 9, 2007, www.worldnetdaily.com/index.php?pageId=42458.

2. Richard Johnson, "Rip-Roaring Rib-Wreckers," March 13, 2009, http://www.nypost.com/seven/03132009/gossip/pagesix/rip_roaring_rib_wreckers_159314.htm.

3. Matthew Belloni, "What I've Learned: Bob Barker," *Esquire*, June 2007.

OFFICIAL CHUCK NORRIS FACT #53

1. Brett and Alex Harris, *Do Hard Things: A Teenage Rebellion Against Low Expectations* (Colorado Springs: Multnomah, 2008), 25. Also visit www.therebelution.com.

OFFICIAL CHUCK NORRIS FACT #54

1. For more on Thomas Jefferson's intermixing of religion and politics, see www.NationalTreasures.org.

2. Dave and his wife, Susie, are to be commended for twenty-six years of sacrifice in Dave's service to the Golden State and our country.

OFFICIAL CHUCK NORRIS FACT #56

1. Quoted in Chuck Norris, "Time for TEA and a Fair Tax," *HumanEvents.com*, April 14, 2009, http://www.humanevents.com/article.php?id=31456.

2. *Fair Tax*, http://www.fairtax.org.

3. James Madison, "Address to the States," 1783.

OFFICIAL CHUCK NORRIS FACT #60

1. Tom Brokaw, *The Greatest Generation* (New York: Random House, 2001), front flap.

2. Isaac Newton, Letter to Robert Hooke, February 5, 1675.

OFFICIAL CHUCK NORRIS FACT #62

1. "How undergraduate students use credit cards: Sallie Mae's national study of usage rates and trends, 2009," *SallieMae.com*, http://www.salliemae.com/about/news_info/research/credit_card_study/.

2. Dave Ramsey, "The truth about debt," *DaveRamsey.com*, http://www.daveramsey.com/the_truth_about/debt_3036.html.cfm.

3. Dave Ramsey, "The truth about credit card debt," *DaveRamsey.com*, http://www.daveramsey.com/the_truth_about/credit_card_debt_3478.html.cfm.

4. "Money Statistics," *Legacy Educational Resources*, http://www.character-education.info/Money/money-studies-and-statistics.htm.

5. "Credit Card Statistics," *CardRatings.com*, http://www.cardratings.com/creditcardstatistics.html.

6. Paul Tharp, "Senate targets abuses by credit card firms," *The New York Post*, January 26, 2007, http://www.nypost.com/seven/01262007/business/senate_targets_abuses_by_credit_card_firms_business_paul_tharp.htm.

7. Romans 13:8, NIV

OFFICIAL CHUCK NORRIS FACT #64

1. David Barton, "Affidavit in Support of the Ten Commandments," *Wall Builders*, January 3, 2001. http://www.wallbuilders.com/LIBissuesArticles.asp?id=87.

2. "The Fifty States Reference God in Their Constitutions—Truth!" *TruthOrFiction.com*, http://www.truthorfiction.com/rumors/g/god-constitutions.htm.

3. Daniel Burke, "Religious citizens more involved—and more scarce?" *USA Today*, May 14, 2009, http://www.usatoday.com/news/religion/2009-05-14-church-community_N.htm

OFFICIAL CHUCK NORRIS FACT #65

1. See www.kickstartkids.org and www.ufaf.org.

2. See http://www.ufaf.org/school_page.asp.

OFFICIAL CHUCK NORRIS FACT #67

1. Joshua 1:9, NASB

2. Revelation 21:4, NIV

3. A foundation in honor of Nick has been set up at http://www.nicholasyancynischanfoundation.blogspot.com.

4. Quoted in Allen Klein, *The Courage to Laugh: Humor, Hope, and Healing in the face of Death and Dying* (New York: J. P. Tarcher/Putnam: 1998), 4.

OFFICIAL CHUCK NORRIS FACT #69

1. "Walter Scott's Personality Parade, *Parade*, April 10, 2007, http://www.parade.com/articles/editions/2007/edition_04-22-2007/Personality_Parade.

OFFICIAL CHUCK NORRIS FACT #73

1. For a list of the top ten reasons to buy American, see http://www.madeinusaforever.com/toptenreasons.html.
2. "Facts for Business," *Federal Trade Commission*, http://www.ftc.gov/bcp/edu/pubs/business/adv/bus03.shtm.
3. I recommend www.madeinusaforever.com or www.stillmadeinusa.com.
4. Lydia Saad, "Putting a Premium on American-Made Products," Gallup News Service, October 18, 2007, http://www.gallup.com/poll/102058/Putting-Premium-AmericanMade-Products.aspx. The comparison in the Gallup survey was between products made in America vs. products made in China. The percentage of Americans willing to pay more for American-made products varied by product category, ranging from 50 percent up to 94 percent: electronics (50%), clothes (60%), shoes (63%), furniture (76%), toys (82%), food (94%).
5. Alex Williams, "Love It? Check the Label," *New York Times*, September 6, 2007, http://www.nytimes.com/2007/09/06/fashion/06made.html?_r=1.
6. "Star Spangled Laughs: A Conversation with Jon Stewart," *Amazon.com*, http://www.amazon.com/gp/feature.html?docId=542410.

OFFICIAL CHUCK NORRIS FACT #74

1. Aaron Barnhart, "Conan O'Brien, the new mayor of late-night, meets and greets," *PopMatters*, March 30, 2009, http://www.popmatters.com/pm/article/72460-conan-obrien-the-new-mayor-of-late-night-meets-and-greets.

OFFICIAL CHUCK NORRIS FACT #75

1. Mike Huckabee, *Quit Digging Your Grave with a Knife and Fork* (New York: Center Street, 2005).

OFFICIAL CHUCK NORRIS FACT #76

1. Department of Public Relations and Marketing Communications for the University of Michigan Health System. "Kids' obesity not weighing on their parents' minds," online report: http://www.med.umich.edu/opm/newspage/2007/poll6.htm.
2. Ibid.; "Overweight and Obesity," *Centers for Disease Control and Prevention*, http://www.cdc.gov/nccdphp/dnpa/obesity.
3. *Divine Health*, http://www.drcolbert.com.

OFFICIAL CHUCK NORRIS FACT #78

1. "Jefferson Memorial (Quotations)," *TH: Jefferson Encyclopedia*, http://wiki.monticello.org/mediawiki/index.php/Quotations_on_Jefferson_Memorial.

OFFICIAL CHUCK NORRIS FACT #79

1. Barna Update, "America's Seven Faith Tribes Hold the Key to National Restoration," April 27, 2009. Barna identifies the seven faith tribes as Casual Christians (66% of the adult population); Captive Christians (16%); Jews (2%); Mormons (2%); Pantheists (2%); Muslims (one-half of 1%); and Skeptics (11%).
2. Barna's diagnosis of America is that "the fundamental disease is a loss of moral and spiritual equilibrium—a decay of our character." He therefore concludes that, although the seven faith tribes are fundamentally different in theology and practice, they share common goals and values that have historically served as the means to achieve national decency and civility—and a good global standing.
3. Government isn't the answer for restoring morality and decency. And neither is education, at least not without religion. As Benjamin Rush, also a signer of the Declaration of Independence, explained, "Without religion, I believe that learning does real mischief to the morals and

principles of mankind" (Benjamin Rush, letter to John Armstrong, March 19, 1783).

4. We, on the other hand, live in a time when we've accepted Washington's challenge, pampered the presumption, and even advocated morality without religion. For we live in a culture in which prayer has been eighty-sixed from schools and civic ceremonies, the Ten Commandments have been sandblasted from our public buildings, creationism has been replaced by evolution, the phrase "In God we trust" is "accidentally" left off the minting of our coins, our Christian heritage is being removed from our historic landmarks (www.NationalTreasures.org), and "under God" is in danger of being removed from the Pledge of Allegiance. The full text of Washington's farewell address can be found online at http://avalon.law.yale.edu/18th_century/washing.asp.

5. Dagobert D. Runes, ed., *The Selected Writings of Benjamin Rush* (New York: Philosophical Library, 1947), 88.

OFFICIAL CHUCK NORRIS FACT #81

1. Jesse Kornbluth, "Q&A: Denzel Washington, Good Guy," *Reader's Digest*, June 2009.

OFFICIAL CHUCK NORRIS FACT #82

1. "Historical Debt Outstanding—Annual 1791–1849," *Treasury Direct*, http://www.treasurydirect.gov/govt/reports/pd/histdebt/histdebt_histo1.htm.

2. See Jefferson quotes on "Money and Banking" at http://etext.virginia.edu/jefferson/quotations/jeff1325.htm.

3. Thomas Jefferson, letter to Samuel Kercheval, 1816, http://etext.virginia.edu/jefferson/quotations/jeff1340.htm.

4. Thomas Jefferson, letter to Alexander Donald, 1787, http://etext.virginia.edu/jefferson/quotations/jeff1325.htm.

OFFICIAL CHUCK NORRIS FACT #86

1. Matthew 20:26-28, NLT

2. Sharon Jayson, "More parents share the workload when mom learns to let go," *USA Today*, May 4, 2009, http://www.usatoday.com/life/lifestyle/2009-05-04-equal-parenting_N.htm.

3. *Ed Cole Library*, http://www.edcole.org and *Majoring in Men*, http://www.majoringinmen.com.

OFFICIAL CHUCK NORRIS FACT #88

1. Thomas Jefferson, *Jefferson: Political Writings*, ed. Joyce Oldham Appleby and Terrence Ball (Cambridge: Cambridge University Press, 1999), 394.

2. See 1 Corinthians 3:16-17; 6:19.

3. Quoted in Chuck Norris, *Black Belt Patriotism: How to Reawaken America* (Washington, D.C.: Regnery Publishing, Inc., 2008), 154.

OFFICIAL CHUCK NORRIS FACT #89

1. "Citizenship in a Republic," speech at the Sorbonne, Paris, April 23, 1910.

OFFICIAL CHUCK NORRIS FACT #90

1. Luke 19:10, NLT

OFFICIAL CHUCK NORRIS FACT #92

1. Lee's fame was crowned with the *Green Hornet* television series. He was then immortalized with such movies as *Enter the Dragon* and *Return of the Dragon*, in which Lee and I fought in the now-famous fighting sequence inside the Roman Colosseum.

OFFICIAL CHUCK NORRIS FACT #93

1. Dr. Gary Smalley, "Building Marital Security in a Culture of Divorce," *Crosswalk.com*, http://www.crosswalk.com/marriage/11549832/.

OFFICIAL CHUCK NORRIS FACT #94

1. 1 Timothy 6:17, NLT

OFFICIAL CHUCK NORRIS FACT #96

1. Letter to Peter Carr, 1785.
2. See http://www.cancer.gov/cancertopics/pdq/supportivecare/ spirituality/Patient/page3; http://nccam.nih.gov/news/newsletter/ 2005_winter/prayer.htm; and http://www.mayoclinic.com/health/ stress-relief/SR00035.
3. *LifeWay Research Insights*, April 16, 2009, http://www.viewsite.org/ Gary/Archives/MAY%2010_09.html. Percentages are 63% among females and 44% among males. Those with whom others shared a Bible truth were: 80% of African-Americans, 46% of Hispanics, and 37% of Asians and Pacific Islanders. Among those who experienced this biblical sharing were 41% of those 65 and older, 57% of 50- to 64-year-olds, 53% of 35- to 49-year-olds, 60% of 25- to 34-year-olds and 51% of 18- to 24-year-olds. In the last six months, 46% of those living with a partner have heard such biblical truths, as well as 52% of married folks and 56% of singles.
4. Proverbs 3:5, 8, NLT
5. Matthew 4:4, NLT
6. You can read *Our Daily Bread* online at http://www.rbc.org/odb/odb .shtml.

OFFICIAL CHUCK NORRIS FACT #97

1. *MovieGuide*, Vol. XXIV, May/June 2009. Also see http://www .movieguide.org/.

OFFICIAL CHUCK NORRIS FACT #99

1. Lindsey Burke, "How Members of the 111th Congress Practice Private School Choice," *The Heritage Foundation*, http://www.heritage.org/ Research/Education/bg2257.cfm.
2. Ibid. The report explains that during the 2007 and 2008 legislative sessions, forty-four states introduced school-choice legislation. In 2008, choices for private schools were enacted into law or expanded in Arizona, Utah, Georgia, Florida, Louisiana, and Pennsylvania. As of 2009, fourteen states and Washington, D.C., offer voucher or education

tax-credit programs that aid parents in sending their children to private schools. What's amazing, too, is how hypocritical it is for Congress to make this decision. The Heritage Foundation report also conveyed that 44 percent of current United States senators and 36 percent of current members of the U.S. House of Representatives "had at one time sent their children to private school." While the Foundation found that 11 percent of American students attend private schools, twice that rate (20 percent) of the members of the 111th Congress attended private schools. And they want to remove the voucher option for private-school education?

3. Get a free chapter of my book at http://www.ChuckNorrisOffer.com.

4. Julia Reynolds, "Olmos On Fire," *El Andar* magazine, Winter 1998; http://www.elandar.com/back/winter98/stories/olmos.html.

OFFICIAL CHUCK NORRIS FACT #101

1. Acts 16:30-34, NIV

2. Randy Alcorn, "The Gift of Hope," *Eternal Perspective Ministries,* http://www.epm.org/artman2/publish/christian_living_discipleship/The_Gift_of_Hope.shtml. Check out all of my friend Randy's resources at www.epm.org.

At the beginning of the Chuck Norris Facts proliferation, I wasn't quite sure what to make of the hundreds (then thousands) of outrageous sayings about my life and legend. I soon realized, however, that in a stress-filled world, these superheroic sayings served to bring smiles and laughs to millions, from school classrooms and college dormitories to corporate offices and the battlefields of war.

So, the way I see it, I have at least a few hundred million people to thank for this book.

To the tens of thousands who have created the Chuck Norris Facts, I'm truly amazed at your creativity. (Okay, most of the time.)

To the hundreds of thousands of students who served as a catalyst for this movement, thank you for reintroducing me to entirely new generations. (I hope the Facts gave you more energy than those high-octane caffeinated drinks to get you through your classes.)

To the millions who have e-mailed, blogged, or in some format posted a Fact, I'm grateful and humbled. (But did you really have nothing better to do?)

To our military servicemen and servicewomen around the world, I'm most grateful that you could use these Facts to bring levity in times of hardship and during your separation from loved ones. (After making two trips to the Middle East, I'll never be able to enter into an outhouse again without picturing in my mind's eye a Chuck Norris Fact on the wall.)

To all the great people at Tyndale House Publishers, thank you for making this manuscript a reality and bringing so much joy to this journey. (Will you sign a copy of the book for me?)

To my family and friends, thanks for still laughing after years of hearing others recite to you and me their favorite Chuck Norris Facts.

To God, for truly understanding that there is really only a simple Southern man at the heart of all those amazing Facts.

Todd A. DuBord is the chaplain of Top Kick Productions. He is also a speaker, writer, and Chuck and Gena Norris's pastor and friend. Todd accompanied Chuck to Iraq in September 2007, where they visited fifteen military bases and more than eighteen thousand troops. He received his BA from Bethany University and an MDiv from Fuller Theological Seminary. Todd has worked for a variety of ministries and has been nationally recognized for his work to restore and preserve America's Judeo-Christian heritage at historic sites and landmarks such as the Washington Monument. Todd and his wife, Tracy, have been married for twenty-six years and have two adult children. You can visit his Web site at www .nationaltreasures.org to hear or download his messages and to learn more about his work to preserve America's religious roots.

KICK**START**

KIDS

**BUILDING STRONG MORAL CHARACTER
IN OUR YOUTH THROUGH MARTIAL ARTS**

To learn more about **KICKSTART KIDS**,
go to **www.kickstartkids.org**.

To contact Chuck Norris,
go to his official Web site:
www.chucknorris.com.

A share of the proceeds from this book
will be donated to **KICKSTART KIDS**.

CP0356

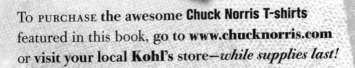

To PURCHASE the awesome **Chuck Norris T-shirts** featured in this book, go to **www.chucknorris.com** or **visit your local Kohl's store**—*while supplies last!*

CP0357